E. H. (Edward Hayes) Plumptre

**Movements in Religious Thought**

Romanism, Protestantism, Agnosticism : Three sSrmons, Preached Before the

University of Cambridge in the Lent Term, 1879

E. H. (Edward Hayes) Plumptre

**Movements in Religious Thought**

*Romanism, Protestantism, Agnosticism : Three sSrmons, Preached Before the University of Cambridge in the Lent Term, 1879*

ISBN/EAN: 9783744776974

Printed in Europe, USA, Canada, Australia, Japan

Cover: Foto ©Lupo / pixelio.de

More available books at **www.hansebooks.com**

# MOVEMENTS

IN

# RELIGIOUS THOUGHT.

# MOVEMENTS IN RELIGIOUS THOUGHT.

I. ROMANISM.   II. PROTESTANTISM.
III. AGNOSTICISM.

THREE SERMONS, PREACHED BEFORE THE
UNIVERSITY OF CAMBRIDGE IN THE
LENT TERM, 1879.

BY

E. H. PLUMPTRE, D.D.,

PROFESSOR OF DIVINITY IN KING'S COLLEGE, LONDON,
PREBENDARY OF ST PAUL'S, VICAR OF BICKLEY, KENT.

"RESPICE, ASPICE, PROSPICE."

London:
MACMILLAN AND CO.
1879

*[The Right of Translation is reserved.]*

TO

## THE REV. J. POWER, D.D.,

MASTER OF PEMBROKE COLLEGE, AND VICE-CHANCELLOR.

DEAR MR VICE-CHANCELLOR,

I owe the opportunity of preaching these sermons to the favour of the Syndicate of which you are Chairman. I am indebted to you for much personal kindness shewn to one who was previously a stranger. I trust you will allow me thus to connect your name with the discourses, now that they are published at your request, and that of other Members of the University.

I am,

Yours very faithfully,

E. H. PLUMPTRE.

BICKLEY VICARAGE,
*Feb.* 19, 1879.

# CONTENTS.

### SERMON I.—ROMANISM.

#### ECCLES. VII. 10.

Say not thou, What is the cause that the former days were better than these? for thou dost not enquire wisely concerning this . . . . 1

### SERMON II.—PROTESTANTISM.

#### S. MATT. XII. 30.

He that is not with me is against me; and he that gathereth not with me scattereth abroad.

#### S. LUKE IX. 50.

Forbid him not: for he that is not against us is for us . . . . 39

## SERMON III.—AGNOSTICISM.

### ACTS XVII. 23.

I found an altar with this inscription, TO THE UNKNOWN GOD.

### ROM. I. 19.

That which may be known of God is manifest in them . . . . 78

## ECCLES. VII. 10.

*Say not thou, What is the cause that the former days were better than these? for thou dost not enquire wisely concerning this.*

THERE is a strange modernness of thought and feeling in these confessions of the Preacher. That sense of the weariness of a confused and disordered life; that sentence of 'Vanity of vanities' written on all man's pains and pleasures, pursuits and aims[1]; that *blasé* cynicism as to the existence of any true disinterested goodness in man or woman[2]; that absence of any clear faith in the future of Israel or of mankind—all this is divided by a whole

---

[1] Eccles. *passim*.      [2] Eccles. vii. 28.

heaven from the life of patriarchs, prophets, psalmists, with which, as by the seeming accident of history, it is now associated. We seem carried into a time when men were drifting away, under the pressure of new problems and new thoughts, from the moorings of their ancient faith, and had not yet found, in the midst of the wild waves of doubts and difficulties which were surging round them, a safe anchorage or the desired haven. We need not, for our present purpose, enquire into the date and authorship of the Book. Whether it represents the conflict, in the mind of the historical Son of David from whom it purports to proceed, between the traditional faith which he had inherited from his fathers, and the largeness of heart which came from contact with other systems of belief and worship; or belongs, as some have thought, to a far later period in the history of Semitic culture, when the teachers of the Garden and the Porch had brought before the mind of some restless thinker other thoughts of God and life, and the chief end of life, than those which had sustained the souls of an earlier generation[1]; this, at any rate is clear, that the aim and purpose of the book seems to be to portray the shiftings and oscillations of a time when the old order is passing away and the new is not developed in its completeness; when men go to and fro in devious ways, in many wanderings of thought. We hear the "two voices" of Scepticism and Faith[2]; the latter heard in feeble protests, unwilling to let slip the hope which yet it cannot firmly grasp; the former uttering itself in loud reiterated murmurs, that the world is out of joint, that man knows nothing, or but very little, of the whence and whither of his being, that a balanced scepticism and an upright life are well-nigh all that he can aim at as a guide in the tangled intricacies of the labyrinth of life;

[1] The dates that have been assigned to the Book take a sufficiently wide range from circ. B.C. 992, on the assumption of Salomonic authorship, still maintained by many critics, to B.C. 200, as fixed on independent grounds by Hitzig and Mr Tylor.

[2] The words remind us of Tennyson's poem, "The Two Voices," which, taken together with his "Palace of Art," is, practically, though with no apparent consciousness of following in the same track, the best commentary on Ecclesiastes.

that, at the best, he can only fall back on the belief that behind the surface disorders of the world, there is working silently, slowly, surely, an Eternal order, that will one day bring to judgment every secret work, whether it be good or evil. (Eccles. xii. 13, 14.)

It is almost a truism that there have been periods in the history of human thought of which this floating, transitional, unsettled state of feeling has been eminently characteristic. It was so when the old faiths of Greece or Rome had yielded to the subtle and pervading influence of Stoic and Epicurean systems and to the scepticism which was engendered by the conflict of those systems. It was so in the sixteenth century, when mediæval theology came into collision with the revived paganism, and the critical questioning temper of the Renaissance[1]. It was so, in our own country,

[1] The scepticism of the Renaissance period had its chief representatives in Italy among the circle of scholars gathered round Lorenzo de Medici at Florence, and who, after watching the attempts of some of their number, like Mirandola and Ficino, to Platonize Christianity, fell into the general license of thought and life which was rebuked by Savonarola. In Giordano Bruno it found a quasi-pantheistic development. It

in the eighteenth century, when men were led, through utter weariness of Calvinistic and Arminian controversies, of questions about vestments and positions, to the free thought which transformed Anglicans into Latitudinarians, and Presbyterians into Socinians, and led others to a cold and naked Deism[1]. It will hardly be questioned that the times in which we are now living present many analogous phenomena. There is an uneasy feeling

was popularized by Montaigne in France, and has left traces of its influence in England in the teaching as to the indifference of Creeds against which the Eighteenth Article of the Church of England is a protest.

[1] Chillingworth is memorable as the leader of the vanguard in this progress to a wider range of thought than that which had been dominant, in one phase under Whitgift and Abbot, in another under Laud. Stillingfleet, Taylor, Burnet, Tillotson, represent its later development within the Church of England. Baxter, in his later years, cast off much of the dogmatism of his earlier life, and became the forerunner of the movement which culminated in the great Conference of Presbyterians, Independents and Baptists at Salter's Hall in 1721, when the first of these three bodies for the first time rejected the principle of subscription to Creeds and Articles, and committed itself to the current of speculative thought which ended in transforming nearly the whole body into the modern Unitarians. Of the wide scepticism of the time Mr Pattison's paper on the "Tendencies of Religious Thought in England, 1688—1792," in *Essays and Reviews*, gives the best accessible account.

that we are living in a transition state and that an unknown future is opening to us. Two great religious movements, tending in opposite directions, have run their course, and seem, in part at least, to have lost their earlier strength. Criticism has opened new fields of enquiry as to the authority of the sacred books, and the nature and measure of the inspiration which men had hitherto ascribed to all alike with an unquestioning reverence. The science which deals with the organic world has opened vistas of a boundless past of almost illimitable æons, during which man and the dwelling-place of man have been alike evolved from lower and more rudimentary forms. The science which deals with the history of human thought has traced a like evolution in the religious history of mankind, and notes affinities between systems of faith and worship where before we had only recognised contrasts. We learn to talk of Semitic tendencies where before we accepted a revelation of the Lord. From many quarters and in many different voices, some grave with the serenity of wisdom, some flippant with the superficial levity of a half-knowledge, we are told that we have ignorantly worshipped—dreaming of Him—or It—as even such an One as ourselves—that which after all must remain for ever as the Unknown and Unknowable, and which there is now no Prophet or Apostle to declare to us. Within the circle of those who have not as yet listened to the voice of the charmer, who would fain stop their ears to the unwelcome words that rob them of their vision of peace and seem to lead them only to the blank darkness of the abyss, there is yet a sense of disquietude and distress. They ask, as they look back upon the past, each school from its own standpoint, contrasting it with the present, why the former days were better than the latter. They sigh for the golden age of faith in which their fathers had rested, trusting in the guidance of the Book that could not err, or in that of its equally infallible interpreter[1].

[1] It is needless to give references for the verification of phenomena which meet our eyes at every turn in the floating literature of the day. It would be enough to give a broad-

It is at once a necessity and a duty at such a time, for those who take any higher view of life than that of acquiescence in the routine of the little world in which they live, to look before and after, to choose their own path, and endeavour to solve, or to recognise as insoluble, the problems which they have to face. The question, Who will shew us any good? is one which many hearts are asking. The work of the preacher, now, as in the days of Ecclesiastes, is to answer that question as of the ability which God giveth, reading, as far as he may, the lessons of the past, recognising the facts of the present, looking forward to that future which in its dim uncertainties awaits alike communities and individual souls. The *Respice, Aspice, Prospice* of St Bernard may well be taken as a watchword both for the speakers and the hearers at such a time and in such a

cast *passim* over the whole ground occupied by the *Nineteenth Century*, the *Westminster*, *Contemporary* and *Fortnightly Reviews*, and the *Pall Mall Gazette*. The nobler leaders of thought will be recognised as I may have occasion to cite their actual words.

place as this. And recognising what are, at least, the dominant forces that are acting upon you to whom I speak, and drawing you in this or that direction, the survey which those words imply will bring before us in succession the systems which represent the two great divisions of Christian thought, with which we are practically concerned, and the forms of thought which lie outside the range of Christendom and which present themselves in the form either of positive denial or of an Agnostic scepticism. Romanism, Protestantism, Unbelief will come before us, that we may ask what claims each has on our regard, what lessons the history of each teaches—what course it is our wisdom to take in regard to each of them.

One word, however, has to be said before we enter on that enquiry, and it concerns us all very nearly. The warning of the preacher, "Thou dost not enquire wisely concerning these things," though we may not accept it blindly as shutting out all such trains of thought as profitless, is not without significance. It is wise to learn the lessons which God has taught mankind through the experience of the past—wise to remember that even the systems of theology which men have deduced from Scripture, or which have been developed by influences apart from Scripture, require to be tested and tried by the teaching of the history of the Church of Christ. It is not wise that we should enter on that enquiry in the temper of a regretful idolatry of the past, or forget that we are called to live and act in the present. Each one of us belongs to a nation, a Church, a College, a neighbourhood, a family, in which, however limited the range of his influence, he may be a power for evil or for good. Each one of us has an earthly life which is capable of growth and discipline till it ripens into life eternal or ends in the shame and misery of an eternal failure. Each has been called to inherit the blessing of being a child of God, redeemed by the blood of Christ from the vain and fruitless life which would otherwise have been his portion. And if as yet, in the doubt and perplexity of these latter times, which we feel to be not better but worse than the former, we fail to grasp these higher thoughts, and they, too, seem to float in the cloudland of dreams and speculations, this, at least, you know and feel, that there lies before every one of you, at every moment of his life, the power of speaking truth and falsehood, of doing good or evil, of feeling love or hatred, and there is a voice within your souls—speaking, as the Master spoke of old, "with authority and not as the scribes[1]," bidding you to refrain from the evil and to seek the good: at least, giving its warnings, even if you do not see how they are to be fulfilled, of a judgment which shall render to every man according to his works, and bring to

[1] The philosophy of Kant is, perhaps, less studied now than it was some forty or fifty years ago. Yet it is well to recall the stress laid by him on the 'categorical imperative,' the authoritative command, *Thou shalt* or *Thou shalt not*, heard in the depths of consciousness as the foundation of all ethics, and to remember that his teaching on this point was recognised by Dr Pusey (*Historical Enquiry*, p. 165) as "an initiating instructor" (the παιδάγωγος of Gal. iii. 24) "leading men to Christ."

light the counsels of all hearts. The life of an unwilling scepticism ought to be more than most lives, one of honest labour, and self-reverencing purity, and thoughtful care for others—for that such a life is true and noble is the one gleam of light which it has to guide it in the tangled labyrinth in which its lot is cast. It is not without a deep significance that the counsels of the preacher who had, far back in the history of thought, anticipated the doubt and weariness of these later ages should be summed up in the rule of life, "Whatsoever thy hand findeth to do, do it with thy might." "Fear God and keep His commandments, for that is all that man has to do[1]." For those who cannot as yet rise to the higher laws: "Do all to the glory of God," "do all in the name of the Lord Jesus[2]," those twin precepts may well be received as being, what indeed they are, oracles of God.

I return to the main enquiry which now lies before us. We ask, as we look back

---

[1] Eccles. ix. 10, xii. 13.   [2] 1 Cor. x. 31; Col. iii. 17.

upon the past history of Christendom—upon the records of the last three hundred years of our own branch of Christendom, upon the currents of thought and feeling within the horizon of our own lives, what is the secret of the power exercised by that system which seems from one standpoint to belong to the former things that have passed away, and from another to retain an unexhausted vitality of existence? What, we ask, is the spring and source of this renewed energy? What are the attractions and what the claims of the Church of Rome on us who are not her children—with what convictions, sympathies, hopes or fears, should we look on her teaching and her policy?

We may enter on that enquiry without bitterness and without prejudice. There is no need for opening old wounds or reiterating the phrases which belong to a time of controversy when men wrote and spoke in the heat of a passionate conflict. "Idolatry to be abhorred of all faithful Christians," "blasphemous fables and dangerous deceits," the exclusion from the heavenly Jerusalem of all who do not forsake what we look upon as the mystical Babylon[1]—these we may well regard as involving more than we would willingly say now in the light of a wider experience and a larger charity. They keep their place in our formularies, because it is not easy to alter them without the risk of a process which might be destructive of much besides, and of which we cannot be sure that it would be followed by a wise reconstruction. We may acknowledge freely, while we protest against errors of doctrine, and corrupt worship, and unfounded claims, and unscrupulous intrigue, that Rome has yet been in times past as "the light of the wide West[2]"

[1] Art. XXXI. *Rubric in Communion Office. Homily against Peril of Idolatry*, Part III. Hooker, in his controversy with Travers, appears almost as the earliest champion of wider and more charitable thoughts (Walton's *Life*, ed. Keble, I. p. 56). There are, I imagine, few bishops or theologians of repute who would willingly use such language now.

[2] The words have the interest of coming from an early poem of J. H. Newman's:

"And next a mingled throng besets the breast
  Of bitter thoughts and sweet;
How shall I name thee, 'light of the wide West';
  Or 'heinous error-seat'?"  *Lyra Apostolica*, CLXX.

—the home of saints—leading many souls to Christ. She, too, has had her martyrs and confessors who did not count their lives dear unto them so that they might finish their course with joy; her mission preachers who have carried the cross of Christ into far-off heathen lands; her witnesses to holiness and purity and humility and love, who have been as lights shining in the world. To admit all this is to make no fatal or unwise concession. For not even this, though it may show that truth has not been altogether lost nor the grace of God's Spirit forfeited, can turn error into truth, or change the weight of evidence, or be accepted as a set-off against manifold corruptions.

There can be little doubt that, at least in these latter times, the secret of the fascination which Rome has exercised even on men of widest culture and subtlest intellect, still more on those who are weak and ignorant and unstable, is found in the prevalent scepticism which marks a period of transition. It is not a happy, hardly even a pleasant, state to be in for one who is conscious of a craving after truth, who would fain have something certain to rest on—who yearns, it may be, for a greater measure of assurance than is compatible with the limits of our knowledge. To that appetite—sometimes healthy, sometimes morbid—Rome appeals. She assumes that it is the purpose of God not only that each soul should have sufficient light for its guidance, if it will live by the light it has, through the chances and changes, the duties and dangers of our life, but that there should be for all the means of attaining to an unerring judgment on all questions which the speculative intellect may raise as to the being of God and His dealings with mankind. And she claims, almost as if the very magnitude of the claim carried with it its own attestation, to give that unerring guidance. She points to the infinite variations of creed among those who rest on Scripture only as a proof that there is no adequate certainty to be found there. In her latest developments she abandons the appeal to an unbroken tradition, and to the authority of the Church as represented in her councils, and rests on the personal infallibility of the so-called successors of St Peter, speaking *ex cathedrâ*, as the one rock on which our faith can rest in the midst of the wild whirling sea of conflicting theories and doubts. "*Roma locuta est; causa finita est*" are her last words to the nations and Churches of Christendom. Beyond her limits, there is no safety; scarcely, except on the plea of invincible ignorance and uncovenanted mercies, the shadow of a hope[1].

We ask, unless we are fascinated by the very magnitude of the claim, on what grounds it rests, and we find that the evidence offered is at every stage inadequate. There is the promise made to Peter, and it is assumed that he is the rock on which the Church was to be

[1] The language, and perhaps the thoughts, of Romish divines has of late shewn that the *Zeit-Geist* has penetrated even where the doors and windows were most closely barred against it, and in their hands, as in those of Anglicans, the plea of "involuntary ignorance and invincible prejudice" is tolerably elastic. It must not be forgotten, however, that the dogma against which the whole of Chillingworth's *Religion of Protestants* was directed was that "Protestantism unrepented of destroys salvation."

built, that he and not Christ is the foundation and the chief corner-stone[1]. It is assumed

[1] Matt. xvi. 18, 19. I may perhaps venture to quote the substance of a note giving what seems to me the true meaning of what has been for centuries the subject of endless controversies. "What then is the rock ($\pi\acute{\epsilon}\tau\rho\alpha$) which is distinguished from the man ($\pi\acute{\epsilon}\tau\rho\text{o}\varsigma$)? Was it Peter's faith (subjective), or the truth (objective) which he confessed, or lastly, Christ Himself? Taking all the facts of the case, the balance seems to incline in favour of the last view: (1) Christ, and not Peter, is the Rock in 1 Cor. x. 4, the Foundation in 1 Cor. iii. 11, the Corner-stone in Eph. ii. 10, and in St Peter's own teaching (1 Pet. ii. 6, 7). (2) The poetry of the Old Testament associated the idea of the Rock with the greatness and steadfastness of God, not with that of a man (Deut. xxxiii. 4, 18; 2 Sam. xxii. 3, xxiii. 3; Ps. xviii. 2, 31, 46; Isai. xvii. 10). (3) As with the words which, in their form, present a parallel to these, 'Destroy *this* temple' (John ii. 19); so here, we may believe the meaning to have been indicated by significant look or gesture. The Rock on which the Church was to be built was Christ Himself, in the mystery of that union of the Divine and the Human which had been the subject of St Peter's confession. Had Peter himself been meant, we may add, the simpler form, 'Thou art Peter, and on *thee* will I build my Church,' would have been clearer and more natural. As it is, the collocation suggests an implied contrast; 'Thou art the Rock-Apostle, and yet not *the* Rock on which the Church is to be built. It is enough for thee to have found the Rock, and to have built on the one Foundation.' What follows as to 'the keys of the kingdom of Heaven,' and the power to bind and to loose, is, as is shewn in the notes that follow, equivalent to the recognition of the disciple's faith as qualifying him for the office of a scribe 'instructed for the Kingdom of Heaven, bringing out of his treasure things new and old' (Matt. xiii. 52), declaring, as Hillel and Shammai had declared, but

that that promise conveyed to him a personal infallibility, and that that infallibility was to be transmitted to his successors, and that those successors are to be found only in the Bishops of Rome. The respect paid in the early ages of the Church to the Bishop of the imperial city is transformed into an admission of his absolute authority. The influence exercised by the higher culture and central position of the Church of Rome over the half-barbarous nations of mediæval Christendom—an influence strengthened by what we may freely recognise as a true missionary activity and the witness borne for a divine order against the tyranny of brute force and secular domination—is treated as if it could give the sanction of the *consensus* of at least European Christianity to a fantastic interpretation of Scripture and a false reading of antiquity. The claim resolves itself at last into the *à priori* assumption that there must be an infallible

with a higher authority resting on divine gifts, what precepts of the law or traditions of the elders were, or were not, of permanent obligation." See Bishop Ellicott's *New Testament Commentary* in loc.

guide somewhere, and that the only church which assumes to be such a guide must *ipso facto* be warranted in its assumption. The earth rests on the elephant, and the elephant on the tortoise, and the tortoise rests not on the eternal rock of fact, but on the cloudland of a dream.

The counter argument from scripture or from history shatters the edifice which has been raised on this unsubstantial and shadowy foundation[1]. Whatever prominence may be given to Peter in the history of the Apostolic Church, it is that gained by energy, activity, great gifts and greater love, and not by any freedom from error or supreme authority. No trace of either is found in the primitive re-

[1] His name stands, it is true, at the head of the list of the Twelve in the Synoptic Gospels and the Acts, but that it is but as *primus inter pares*, and that the promise of Matt. xvi. 18 was not thought of as conferring more than this, is shewn by the fact that it was after this that the two sons of Zebedee came with their request to sit at their Lord's right hand and His left in His kingdom (Matt. xx. 20, 21; Mark x. 35), and that there were two disputes which was greatest (Luke ix. 47, xxii. 24). The emphatic words "Many that are first shall be last, and the last first" (Matt. xix. 30), might well seem to rebuke any claim to a personal and permanent primacy of power.

cords of the Church of Christ. The impulsive, wayward disciple during our Lord's ministry on earth, now venturing on the troubled sea, and now sinking through his want of faith[1], uttering words which indicate an almost child-like ignorance of the Lord's mind and purpose[2], denying, in the paroxysm of a coward fear, Him whom he had acknowledged to be the very Son of the living God, having the words of eternal life—this is surely not what we should have pictured for ourselves as the Apostle who was to present to men the type of an unerring steadfastness. The Pentecostal gift brought doubtless to him as to others, but not to him more than others, wider thoughts and a new illumination, but the old vacillation and infirmity remained, and the Apostle by whom the door of faith had been opened to the Gentiles, was condemned alike by the feeling of the Church and by the mouth of one to whom had been given a larger wisdom than his own[3]. In his conferences with that

[1] Matt. xiv. 28—31.
[2] Matt. xv. 15, xvi. 22, xvii. 5, xviii. 21.
[3] "I withstood him to the face, because *he had been condemned* (ὅτι κατεγνωσμένος ἦν)." Gal. ii. 11.

other Apostle he appears as receiving, not as imparting, the full truth of the mystery of God and the universality of His kingdom[1]. In the first great controversy which threatened to break up the unity of the Church there is no appeal, as, on the Roman theory, there should have been, to his decision as final and supreme. He speaks, it is true, wisely and rightly, but it is as one debater among many, and the decision rests not with him, but with the Apostles and elders and the lay members of the Church[2].

It seems almost surplusage of argument to go beyond this, but it may be added, that even if the position of St Peter had been other than it was, there is not one jot or tittle of evidence in the writings of the New Testament or those of the age that followed it, to connect him with the pastoral superintendence of the Church of Rome. The foundation of that Church is traceable not to him or to St Paul but to obscurer and less honoured

---

[1] Gal. ii. 2, 6.

[2] Acts xv. 7, 14, 23. As Peter, according to the Romish hypothesis, had already entered on the years of his Episcopate in the imperial city, this absence of any recognition of his supreme authority is all the more striking.

preachers of the truth, perhaps to Aquila or Andronicus or Junias[1], perhaps to workers of whose very names not a record has come down to us. Had he assumed a supreme authority in that Church he would have been, to use his own expressive term, as an ἀλλοτριοεπίσκοπος[2], a bishop in a diocese not his own, even as those who claim to be his successors have, as in the strange irony of history, shewn themselves to be ἀλλοτριοεπίσκοποι in every Church in Christendom. The history of those

[1] It is a natural inference from the absence of any records of Aquila's conversion, as well as from his immediate readiness to fraternize with St Paul, that he already shared the Apostle's faith, and this at least falls in with the hypothesis, now generally received, that the expulsion of the Jews from Rome was connected with tumults in which the name of Christ (which we recognise in the "*impulsore Chresto*" of Suetonius (Claud. c. 25) had been bandied to and fro between opposing parties. Of Andronicus and Junias we know that they were Roman Christians, and that their conversion to the faith had preceded the conversion of St Paul, and must therefore have been earlier than the persecution which culminated in the death of Stephen (Rom. xvi. 7). The chief opponents of Stephen, it will be remembered, were the *libertini*, or emancipated Jews, and proselytes from Rome who had a synagogue at Jerusalem (Acts vi. 9), and there are some reasons for connecting the martyr himself with the imperial city. See Bishop Ellicott's *Commentary on Acts* vi. 5.

[2] 1 Pet. iv. 15.

successors, the work they have done for good or evil, in the history of the Church is, I need scarcely say, incompatible with the claim. Popes have lapsed into what other Popes have condemned as heresy. They have stultified themselves by flagrant contradictions on facts of criticism or history[1]. Personal vices or a persistent policy of ambition and intrigue may, perhaps, be theoretically compatible with an official infallibility, assuming its existence to be proved, but they are but unsatis-

---

[1] The more familiar cases are those of Liberius, who subscribed the Arian Creed at the third Council of Sirmium (A.D. 357), and Honorius, who was condemned as holding the Monothelite heresy by the sixth General Council at Constantinople (A.D. 680), and by his successor Leo II. Other instances will be found in the volume on *The Pope and the Council* by the writer who took the *nom de plume* of Janus. The advocates of Rome have, of course, a case which they maintain, with more or less ability, against the verdict of history, but the one fact which emerges, even admitting the success of efforts to whitewash the individual Popes, is that no one then dreamt of the office as identified with infallibility. The well-known *Bellum Papale* of the Sixtine and Clementine editions of the Vulgate, each stamped with an *ex cathedrâ* authority, and containing some 3000 variations in their texts, remains as a witness that the claim which had by that time been made could not bear the test of even superficial criticism. (See Dr Westcott's Article, *Vulgate*, in Smith's *Dictionary of the Bible*.)

factory accompaniments of its possession, and are poor credentials of the mission of one who assumes to speak as the oracle of God. If the test " by their fruits ye shall know them" is, in any measure, a true test, there are, at least, many in the long list of Pontiffs who must take their place among the false prophets who are as ravening wolves, and not among the preachers of righteousness and the witnesses for the truth. And it is a singular outcome of the claim to be the one witness and keeper of the Word of God, the one interpreter of its mysteries, that no church in Christendom has done so little for settling the Canon or unfolding the meaning of Scripture as the Church of Rome, that none in that Church have done so little as its long line of Bishops[1]. We might have expected the one pattern-

[1] Chillingworth's answer to the argument drawn by the advocates of Rome from the difficulties of Scripture, and the consequent necessity for some authorized and unerring interpreter, is pointed enough to deserve quotation. If the Pope possesses this power, he asks, why does he not write a Commentary? "Why not seat himself *in cathedrâ*, and fall to writing expositions upon the Bible for the direction of Christians to the true sense of it?" *Religion of Protestants*, I. II. § 95.

scribe instructed to the kingdom to have brought forth from his treasure "things new and old." As a matter of fact he has too often closed the doors of the treasure-house against those who were seeking to enter in; he has brought out, not the pearls and precious stones of truth, but the rubbish of the false Decretals and of wildly fantastic interpretations[1]. The work of settling what books were entitled to canonical authority, what text of those books was authentic, was left in earlier, as in later times, to private judgment, working on the *data* supplied by history and criticism. Councils followed in the wake of

---

[1] No thoughtful student of Scripture will take a low estimate of the work done by many individual interpreters of the Church of Rome. The names of Aquinas and de Lyra, of Maldonatus and Estius, of Cornelius à Lapide and Calmet, are worthy of all honour. But when we pass from these "particular persons," following Butler's method, to the writings of the Bishops of Rome, we have to fall back upon such expositions as we find, e.g. in the Bull "*Unam Sanctam*" of Boniface VIII., in which the "two great lights" of Gen. i. 16 are made to represent the spiritual and temporal powers as impersonated in the Pope and the Emperor, and the *Magna Moralia* of Gregory I., in which the seven sons of Job represent the "*ordo praedicantium*," and his three daughters the "*multitudo audientium*."

scholars and confirmed their decisions[1]. The work of interpretation has from the first been carried on, as it will be to the end, not by Popes or Councils, but by the exercise of the individual intellect guided, in greater or less measure, by the illumining grace of the Eternal Spirit; dwelling on the meaning of the words and the sequence of thoughts, on the character, environment, and purpose of the writer whom we interpret; or, to use Butler's words, "in the same way as natural knowledge is come at, by the continuance and progress of learning and of liberty; by particular persons attending to, comparing and pursuing, intimations scattered up and down it, which are overlooked and disregarded by the generality of the world. For this is the way in which all improve-

[1] When it is said that we receive Scripture on the authority of the Church, it should be remembered that the work of Melito of Sardis, of Origen, of the author of the Muratorian Fragment, of Eusebius of Caesarea preceded the earliest authenticated lists drawn up by the Council of Laodicea (circ. A. D. 363) and the third Council of Carthage (A.D. 397). The actual order is in accordance with the natural course of things, and not with that demanded by a hypothesis: (1) general currency and acceptance, (2) individual scrutiny, (3) authoritative determination.

ments are made; by thoughtful men tracing on obscure hints, as it were, dropped us by nature accidentally, or which seem to come into our minds by chance." (*Anal.* II. 3.)

It cannot be doubted, however, that, as a matter of fact, the Roman Communion has exercised influences of another kind over minds differently constituted from the enquirers who seek simply for intellectual certainty. The long history that stretches back into the remote past—the wide extent of her sway and the apparent unity that rests on her central authority—the stately impressiveness of her ritual, affecting the imagination through the senses and the emotions through the imagination—the provision which she makes for sin-burdened consciences by her system of confession and absolution—the hope which she offers to those who mourn for their dead, of a remedial and purifying discipline after death bringing to completeness the holiness without which no man shall see the Lord, and which, when their earthly course was finished was but incomplete and almost rudimentary—the high ideal of saintly and self-devoted life which has been aimed at and not seldom realised, in her religious communities of men and women—all this, we know but too well, has exercised its power of fascination over weak and unstable natures; sometimes, we must admit, over those whom we could not so describe without an arrogant injustice. But to those who are, in greater or less measure, under the influence of these attractions, we may say that, so far as they are legitimate in their action, they are not the exclusive heritage of Rome, that it is to her misuse of them that we may largely trace the neglect of them which has, it may be, too largely characterised the Churches that have separated from her. It has been one, at least, of the gains, balancing some serious drawbacks, of the so-called Catholic revival of the last fifty years that it has given a brighter and more joyous character to our worship; that it has taught us that Art in all its manifold applications to sight and hearing may legitimately be employed to stir up the dull minds of men to soar heavenwards even on the wings of sense, that we have learnt from it that the highest act of Christian worship, that which is the witness of our communion and fellowship with all who name the name of Christ on earth, and with the saints who have passed to their eternal home, with angels and archangels and all the company of Heaven, need not be in its outward accompaniments the most cold and lifeless act of all[1]. It has led men, if not always wisely, yet with an earnestness which deserves all praise, to feel that the ministry of souls involves something more than sermons however earnest, and calls for the personal con-

---

[1] I am not, of course, defending any special form of ritual, still less any which is at variance with the decisions of the tribunal which, whether we admit the force of its reasonings or not, is for us, as English Churchmen, at least for the present, the authoritative exponent of the Rubrics of the Prayer-Book. But it is impossible to compare the type of worship which now prevails among us with that which was all but universally dominant till within the last forty years, without feeling that there has been a great change for the better, and that this has been wrought out by those who at nearly every stage have had to encounter the brunt of suspicion and distrust, sometimes even of mob violence and irritating prosecutions.

tact of mind with mind and heart with heart, for the outpouring of the confession of the sin-burdened soul and the words of comfort and counsel that bring home to the penitent the assurance of pardon and absolution[1]. It

[1] I have stated elsewhere, in a Sermon on *Confession and Absolution*, the reasons which lead me to look on this element in the work of the ministry as belonging to its prophetical rather than its priestly character. The "drawbacks" to which I refer are, I need scarcely say, the tendency which has shewed itself among those who adopt the practice to follow the guidance of Romish casuists, like Dens or Liguori, rather than that of the wiser masters of the School of Conscience, and to dwell with a minuteness, prurient in its results, if not in its intention, as in the too conspicuous instance of the *Priest in Absolution*, on the "things done in secret," of which "it is a shame to speak." That tendency one may deplore and protest against, but in the popular outcry raised on the strength of it against the practice of Confession, from the journalism of the Clubs and the oratory of platforms to the street-hawkers of pamphlets with suggestive extracts, I find nothing that can deserve our sympathy, much that I cannot regard as other than the product of the hypocrisy which is content that the things in question should be done so long as they are not spoken of. It is not an exaggeration to say that there is a greater element of corruption in any one of the thousand provincial newspapers which are published, week by week, without let or hindrance, than in the work which became a nine days' wonder. It is surely an unsatisfactory outcome of Protestantism that it should prefer that those who have fallen into sensuous sins should "open their grief" to the counsellors who thus invite their confidence rather than pour out their sorrow and shame to the ministers of Christ. See an interesting Article on *Confession* by Dr Cornell in the *Contemporary Review* for March, 1879.

has in many ways revived the idea and the practice of associated and consecrated labour for God's glory and the good of men in fraternities and sisterhoods and guilds, without the snare of vows of perpetual obligation. It has given a new impetus to the Church's mission work, both as evangelising the heathen in far-off lands and preaching Christ to those who, though they live and die under the very shadow of the Churches, have lapsed into a practical heathenism and need to be taught what are the first principles of the oracles of God. Mingling with a current of thought, which in its main drift, started from a different quarter, and flows in an opposite direction, it has led us to look into the dim region that lies behind the veil with a wider hope than our fathers dared to cherish, and to believe that there also, wherever there is yet the capacity for a higher life, the everlasting Love is not willing that any should perish but that all should come to repentance[1].

---

[1] I refer, of course, to the "wider hope" which cherishes the thought that the education of the soul, that it may be fit

No, we do ill, even looking at Rome on her best and brightest side, to ask impatiently and unwisely, why the former days were better than the latter. And, on the other side of the account, she comes before the tribunal of History and of Truth heavily weighted with many serious charges from which even the subtlest eloquence of her advocates will find it hard to clear her. She has darkened counsel by words without knowledge, and in her endeavours to formulate the fact of Christ's spiritual presence with His people, has overshadowed it with the cumbrous theories of substance and accidents that belong to an obsolete philosophy. She has pushed those theories to their logical result in practice, and has called men to acts of adoration, of which it is hard to say, even while we shrink from the harsh words of condemnation which our

for the mansions of its Father does not cease at the moment of death, and that there may be behind the veil new stirrings of repentance and apprehensions of the truth and growth in holiness, of which Mr Maurice was, if one may so speak, the proto-martyr, and which has since been advocated in various forms by Mr Wilson, Mr Kingsley, Professor Grote, and Dr Farrar.

fathers thought themselves justified in using in the heat of conflict, that they do not bring with them at least the peril of idolatry, *i.e.* of the substitution of the symbol for the thing symbolised, of a sensuous for a spiritual worship. She has taught men practically to trust to the intercession, the patronage, the protection of created mediators who, in their turn, have been presented as objects of devotion through outward forms, in painting or in sculpture[1]. She has by her doctrine of

---

[1] The "*Monstra te esse Matrem*" of the hymn in the Office of the Blessed Virgin is strong enough as an illustration of the tendency of which I speak, but it has been shewn that it is but as the germ of a monstrous growth of Mariolatry which is practically becoming more and more *the* religion of France and Italy and Spain. Proofs enough and to spare may be found in Dr Pusey's *Eirenicon* or an anonymous pamphlet, written, I believe, by the late Rev. W. E. Jelf, *A Review of Mariolatry* (Rivingtons, 1869). It is not without interest to note that the extracts given by Dr Pusey from works published with more or less authority from Roman Catholic Bishops, and in wide use throughout their flocks, are enough to move even Dr Newman to language almost as strong as any Protestant could desire: "I consider them calculated to prejudice enquirers, to frighten the unlearned, to unsettle consciences, to provoke blasphemies, to work the loss of souls....I know not to what authority to go for them—to Scripture, or to the Holy Fathers, to the decrees of Councils, or to the consent of Schools, or to the tradition of the faithful, or to reason" (*Letter to Dr Pusey*, pp. 120, 121).

purgatory and her practice of indulgences turned the Gospel message of pardon and peace into a narcotic for the conscience—not seldom into a source of ill-gotten gain and an instrument of spiritual oppression. She has accustomed men to a worship in a speech which they cannot understand, into which they at least cannot enter with the fulness of thought and speech which is found only when men pray in the language in which they think, and, as if reversing the Pentecostal wonder, has decreed that they should not hear, every man in his own tongue, wherein they were born, the wonderful works of God. If Protestant Churches and sects have shared with her, as they have but too largely shared, in the guilt of a persecuting intolerance, upon her rests the blame of having led the way, of having made men accept almost as an axiom, from which it required centuries of freedom to clear their 'long-abused vision,' that religious error is a crime, to be punished like other crimes, of having carried that principle age after age to results by the side of which all other acts of persecution dwindle into insignificance[1].

[1] The first blood shed in the name of religious truth was, it may be noted, that of Priscillian, a Spanish Bishop, who had embraced some form of Manichaean or Gnostic opinion, and was put to death by the usurper Maximus (A.D. 385). The employment of the civil sword was condemned in strong and earnest terms by St Ambrose and St Martin of Tours, the former of whom refused to communicate with the Bishops who had been the advisers of the act or sharers in it. The Bishop of Rome, however, Leo II., sanctioned the fatal principle of recourse to the secular arm. The Church, "quae, etsi sacerdotali contenta judicio, cruentas refugit ultiones, severis tamen Christianorum principum constitutionibus adjuvatur, dum ad spiritale nonnunquam recurrunt remedium, qui timent corporale supplicium" (Milman's *Latin Christianity*, B. II. c. 4). In that fatal "*nonnunquam*," that sacrifice of the law of Christ for the chance of an uncertain gain, we find the germ-cell (to return once more to the metaphor naturally suggested by the Theory of Development) out of which have come in terrible succession the slaughter of the Albigenses, the *Auto-da-fés* of Spain, the massacre of St Bartholomew, the fires of Smithfield, the Dragonnades under Louis XIV., the long torturing tyranny of the Inquisition. How hard it was to throw off the incubus of the πρῶτον ψεῦδος we find but too plainly in the action of Anglican Reformers under Henry VIII. and Elizabeth, of Calvin in the execution of Servetus, of Scotch Presbyterians, and the Courts of the Star Chamber and High Commission. Perhaps, however, the crowning instance of the power of the evil demon to return even to the house from which it had been cast out is seen in Chillingworth. He, who in the *Religion of Protestants* had claimed an almost unlimited freedom, and written strongly against the persecuting policy of the Church of Rome, came within a few short years to "count it a greater happiness than God had granted to his chosen ser-

I know not how far any of you may have felt the power of that spell which has fascinated not a few ardent and eager spirits, which has led some to fear and some to hope that the tide was turning, and that the wave which we had watched in its slow retreat for three hundred years, was creeping in again in creeks and bays, and was about to submerge once more many fair fields of thought and action. I have not sought to speak in accents of alarm—still less to urge the policy of jealousy and suspicion, which originates in panic and does but augment the danger. But we cannot close our eyes to the fact that the danger exists. The former days will, in a time of bewilderment and controversy and doubt, seem to some better than the latter. And therefore, I trust I shall not seem to have misused the opportunity which has been given me, by urging those who have listened to the voice of the charmer, to reconsider that

vants in the infancy of the Church that we now have the sword of the civil magistrate, the power and enforcement of laws and statutes, to maintain our precious faith against all heretical and schismatical oppugners thereof" (*Sermons*, II. 15).

conclusion. There is a heavy *onus probandi* on all resolves to abandon the position in which God has placed us before we have made full proof of all the openings it presents for the advancement of our own spiritual life, and the welfare of those among whom we are called to work. England, and the Church which is identified with the life of England, are, for us at least, the Sparta which God has given us to beautify and set in order, and it would be ill done to desert our post and to take our flight on the wings of scepticism into the abysmal depths of superstition.

## II. PROTESTANTISM.

### S. MATT. XII. 30.

*He that is not with me is against me; and he that gathereth not with me scattereth abroad.*

### S. LUKE IX. 50.

*Forbid him not: for he that is not against us is for us.*

IT is obvious that the two utterances which I have read seem, at first sight, to tend in opposite directions. The one might well become the basis of a wider and more comprehensive Catholicity than any Church of Christendom has as yet attained to. The other might appear to sanction the most rigorous measures to enforce uniformity, and to repress every form of schism and dissent. We need, in the enquiry on which we enter to-day, yet more in the part which every one of us will some day have to play in relation to parties within the Church's pale or to sects outside it, to interpret rightly what Bacon has well called these "cross-clauses of the league of Christians[1]." It is, for good or evil, the characteristic feature of Protestantism that it has been fruitful in these variations. It has been marked, if one may so speak, by the hypertrophy of individualism, as the history of the Church of Rome has been marked by its suppression.

It will be noted as a help to a right understanding of our Lord's words that both the passages which I have cited were spoken primarily in connexion with the work of casting out demons. I need not now enter into the vexed question of the nature of that demoniac possession. It is enough for our present purpose to recognise its phenomena without involving ourselves in any disputable theory of causation. Those phenomena are,

[1] Bacon's *Essays*, III. *Of Unity in Religion*.

beyond dispute, identical with many that we now connect with the idea of morbid conditions of brain or nerve, of spiritual states that lie on the very verge of insanity. There is a strange dualism in the nature which should be at unity within itself. Alternate paroxysms of fear and hate, and love and adoration—a preternatural insight and a reckless disregard of the conventional restraints of life—wild or ceaseless cries, or persistent and sullen silence—these are the features that present themselves even to the most superficial reader of the Gospel records[1]. On these our Lord looked as with an infinite compassion, and made it one chief object of His work to heal the evils which thus met His gaze. And it was seen that His word was with power. The disorder was, in the main, spiritual, and yielded to spiritual and not to physical remedies. The loving look—the gracious welcome—the recognition of the true humanity which lay beneath the wild conflict of the legion of

[1] See Trench *on the Miracles*, v. *The Demoniacs in the country of the Gadarenes;* or *Excursus* on Matt. viii. 28 in Bishop Ellicott's *New Testament Commentary*.

tempestuous passions—these had power to cast out the demon forces, and to change the wild howling maniac into a disciple, sitting at the feet of Jesus, clothed and in his right mind; to bring to the fevered spirit the peace and the sweet sleep which no poppies or mandragora could have ministered. And what the Lord Jesus did Himself, that He taught His disciples also to do. It was His first commission to them, that, as they preached the Gospel of the Kingdom, they were to heal the sick and to cast out devils. Their chief ground of joy when they returned was that even the devils were subject to them through His Name. Their exultation had its counterpart in His joy. He saw in this the pledge and earnest of His future victory over the powers of evil—He beheld as in vision Satan, "as lightning, fall from heaven," cast out from his usurped dominion in the "heavenly places" of the mind and will of man[1].

Those who saw or heard of this work looked on it, the Gospel records tell us, with

---

[1] Matt. x. 1; Mark iii. 15; Luke x. 17, 18; Eph. vi. 12.

widely different feelings. The Scribes and Pharisees felt no sympathy with it. It mattered not to them whether the Gadarene demoniac remained in chains and fetters, howling in the tombs, or returned to his own home as in the peace of God. What did matter was that the power was exercised by One who was not of their school and had rebuked their hypocrisy. They stood aghast at the proof thus given of the presence among them of a spiritual power mightier than their own. That it was a spiritual, preternatural power they could not, even from their own stand-point, deny, and they ventured on the horrible paradox that the good work was wrought by the Power of Evil, that the liberation of the human spirit from its bondage had its source in the subtlety of the great oppressor. " He casteth out devils by Beelzebub," was their solution of the problem which presented itself. On the temper that thus judged there was passed the sentence, " He that is not with me is against me, and he that gathereth not with me scattereth abroad." It approximated, with an awful nearness, to the sin of intense persistent antagonism to goodness as such, slandering and resisting it, which, in its ultimate development, excludes forgiveness because it excludes repentance[1]. In the great warfare of Christ against the power of evil, the end and aim of which was to rescue those who had been held as captives, and gather them into His Father's house, there could be no real neutrality. He that did not help to gather, whose heart beat with no yearning sympathy for those who were wandering and lost, was practically perpetuating the isolation and the misery which Christ sought to overcome. On others, however, what they heard of the works of the Christ produced a different impression. It stirred up dormant sympathies and roused into energy powers that had been latent. They too would use the prayer of faith and the Name that was mighty above all names, that so they might deliver those who had, it may be, for long years of their life, been subject unto bondage. They

[1] Matt. xii. 24—32; Mark iii. 22—30; Luke xi. 14—20.

looked on the frenzied demon-haunted souls whom they met, with a compassion like that of Christ. And their words too were mighty and prevailed. Peace and calmness took the place of restless agitation[1]. The man was gathered into the fold of that humanity from which he had strayed into the howling wilderness. Those who so worked had not as yet— we know not for what reason—joined themselves to the company of the disciples that followed Jesus, but they shewed by using His name that they believed in Him, and by the purpose for which they used it that their mind was one with His. And therefore when the disciples sought to make that outward union an essential condition of any recogni-

---

[1] Mark ix. 38; Luke ix. 50. It is obvious that whatever we understand by "casting out devils" was actually accomplished by those whom the disciple (St John) sought to restrain from working. This was true also, it would seem from our Lord's reasoning in Matt. xii. 27; Luke xi. 19, of the "children" or disciples of the Pharisees. To them also, if they were single-minded in their purpose, and used the name of the Most High God, not, like the vagabond exorcists of Ephesus, as a spell or charm, but in humility and faith, prayer brought a spiritual power to deliver which was mighty to prevail against spiritual evil.

tion of those who were thus working, they were met with words, which, under the form of a paradox, presented the opposite pole of the self-same truth. He that was not against Christ in that warfare with evil—who was actually engaged in the conflict, though it might be in skirmishes that lay outside the plan of the regular campaign, was really an ally and not an enemy—to be welcomed, not to be condemned. It was not among such as these that one would be found who would "lightly speak evil" of Him.

The "cross clauses" of the league of Christians are thus seen to receive their practical interpretation, not, as Bacon suggests[1], in

---

[1] Bacon's *Essays*, III. "Both these extremes" (the zeal of the persecutor and Laodicean lukewarmness) "are to be avoided; which will be done, if the league of Christians penned by our Saviour Himself were in the two cross-clauses thereof soundly and plainly expounded, 'he that is not with us is against us,' and again, 'he that is not against us is with us': that is, if the points fundamental, and of substance, in religion, were truly discerned and distinguished from points not merely of faith, but of opinion, order and good intention. This is a thing may seem to many a matter trivial and done already; but if it were done less partially, it would be embraced more generally." The concluding words form a melancholy comment on many memorable passages in the con-

a company of divines sitting round a table and examining which of the formulated afterthoughts of theology are to be classed as essential or non-essential, fundamentals or things indifferent, but in looking to the temper in which men are acting and the work which they are doing. Are they casting out devils, or slandering and thwarting those who do cast them out? Are they warring, to extend the principle in a way which all will surely recognise as legitimate, against the demon passions that desolate and make havoc of all that is best and noblest in man's nature— against lust and hate and falsehood, against pride and injustice and oppression? If so, the word of command still goes forth from the Lord of the Churches, "Forbid them not, for he that is not against us is for us." Are they among the upholders of traditional prejudices, the sneerers at enthusiasm, the

troversies of Christendom. It would have been well for the Church at large, for our own National Church in particular, if this teaching had been more acted on, but there is after all "a more excellent way" even than moderation in fixing "fundamentals."

cavillers at details, among those who never hear of any earnest work for the souls of men without asking the *Cui bono?* of a cynical suspicion? For them, as for those who said of Christ that He cast out devils by Beelzebub, there is the condemnation, "He that is not for us is against us."

The truth thus established is manifestly not without its bearing on our thoughts and feelings, even as to the system of the Church of Rome. There also we find, and may give God thanks that we do find, those who, not without success, have given themselves, in this form or in that, to the work of casting out devils. There also, for the most part in her high places of authority, we find those who have condemned men who were doing that work, almost in the very words in which the Pharisees condemned our Lord. We need, as far as lies in our power, to recognize the distinction between the two classes. Where we find, as in such characters as St Dominic, and Carlo Borromeo, and Francis de Sales[1], a strange blending of the two contrasted elements, a warm tender illumined love of souls mingled with a zeal, not according to knowledge, against the error or the truth which they looked on as hateful heresy, we must be content to leave the judgment which History shrinks from pronouncing, to Him before whom the secrets of all hearts are as an open scroll—from whom even the persecutor may obtain the mercy which he has refused to others, on the ground that he has acted ignorantly and in unbelief, not slighting conscience but misled by an invincible prepossession.

We must feel, however, when we turn from the one vast system with its centralised unity to the manifold sects and parties which popularly come under the common category of

[1] I write the two names not without reluctance, but it must be remembered that both were among the most energetic leaders of the Anti-Reformation party in the sixteenth century, that Borromeo was the main author of the *Catechism* which popularised the teaching of the Council of Trent, and that he brought the Jesuits into Switzerland; and that the 70,000 converts whom the Bishop of Geneva was said to have brought back from the heresy of Calvin to the bosom of the Church were not gained altogether without the use of the secular arm of the Duke of Savoy.

Protestantism, that we need the balanced teaching of the twin precepts more than ever to direct our judgment and to guide our conduct. For you to whom I speak, that is the one chief lesson to be learnt. There is probably not one of you who has felt, or ever will feel, called on to discuss the question whether it is his duty to become a Wesleyan or a Congregationalist. How you are to judge and act towards Wesleyans and Congregationalists is a question which you can scarcely ignore with safety at any stage on your work, as laymen or as clergymen.

I do not care to dwell at length on the question which has been raised, whether the Church of which we are members is itself rightly described as Protestant. Historically it may be true that the epithet is not altogether a happy one. In its origin it had little or no dogmatic significance. In its next stage it implied the acceptance of the Confession of Augsburg as distinct from those of the Reformed Churches of France or Switzerland—agreement with Luther and Melancthon rather than with Calvin and Beza. In the wider range of connotation which it ultimately acquired it expressed little more than the negation of such errors as were distinctive of the Roman Communion. It has never been adopted by the Church of England in any formal statement of her position. If, at one time, it was accepted almost boastfully by some of her most conspicuous teachers— by those even whom we regard as representatives of her more Catholic aspects, by Laud and Cosin no less than by Chillingworth and Tillotson, the title has lost something of its greatness by passing to viler uses[1]. It has

[1] The Edict of Worms (A.D. 1521) had condemned Luther in the strongest possible terms, and ordered rigorous measures to be taken throughout the Empire against him and his followers. At the Diet of Spires (A.D. 1526) the Reforming party obtained an unanimous decree suspending the operation of that Edict, and urging a general Council as necessary for the peace and order of the Church. At the Second Diet of Spires (A.D. 1529) the Anti-Reform party, by a majority, repealed the decree of the First and thus restored the Edict of Worms to full activity. Against this decree six Princes and the deputies of fourteen imperial cities protested, partly on constitutional, partly on religious grounds. The name *Protestants*, first applied to them as so acting, soon spread to their followers. The earliest instance of its wider use beyond the limits of Germany with which I am acquainted

been made the plea for the intolerance of statesmen and the violence of mobs, and the panic and prejudices of the ignorant[1]. Those who were sunk in a life of worldliness, or who looked on the Established Church from a

is in Ridley's speech on his trial: "Yea, I protest, call me Protestant who will." It probably grew in popularity under Elizabeth, and Bacon (*Observations on a Libel*) speaks of the "protestantical Church of England" as though it were a recognised phrase. The title of Chillingworth's book shews that it was adopted by the high Anglican party whom he represented. Charles spoke of himself as a "Protestant king." Laud claimed the title for himself and Andrewes (*Speech on his Trial*). Cosin, in his will, expressed his yearning after outward communion, his actual heart-communion, with foreign "Protestants." The term was struck out of an address presented to William III. by a vote of the Lower House of the Convocation of Canterbury, but retains its place in the Coronation Service in the promise of the Sovereign to maintain the "Protestant religion."

[1] We look back with a half-sad, half-contemptuous wonder at the time when English Protestantism turned to Lord George Gordon, or Lord Eldon, or the Duke of Cumberland as its leaders, when the Duke of York's "So help me God!" speech was printed in letters of gold as if it had been an oracle from heaven. Are we quite certain that we are better than our fathers? The surplice riots at Exeter and St George's in the East, the recent scenes at Hatcham, the organised action of an Association which exists only for the purpose of promoting prosecutions about the "mint, anise and cummin" of obscure and obsolete rubrics, will not be bright spots for the future historians of the nineteenth century to dwell on.

political standpoint, simply as Established, have sheltered themselves under the profession of a zeal for its Protestant doctrines. At the best, the word carries with it a simply negative aspect, and no mere negation can be an adequate bond of unity. There may be something to be said, however unattainable the ideal may be, for the dream of a union of religious societies on the basis of a common Christianity, but the basis of a common Protestantism is, of all things, the most shadowy and unsubstantial. We may feel, as indeed we ought to feel, respect and gratitude for those who, in past times, bore the burden and heat of a conflict in which we too were sharers, but an alliance, offensive and defensive, requires, as a condition of permanence, something more than hostility to a common foe. We may recognise, with no grudging acceptance of the fact, that the tone of the dogmatic formularies of the Church of England is eminently protestant against the errors of that of Rome. We do well to avoid all supercilious scorn in our treatment of a word which was once honourable, and stirred the hearts of men like a trumpet, calling them to battle, but we need to add another term to it in order that it may define our position with any adequacy. Catholic first, and then because Catholic, protestant against the counterfeit of Catholicity, is the only legitimate description of the position which our Church occupies in its relation to this controversy.

Leaving this question of words and names, we pass on to ask what have been the main characteristics for good or evil, of those to whom, as having these at least, in common, the name of Protestant has been applied; how far it is in our power to refuse the evil and to choose the good; how we ought to deal with those who seem to us to have chosen the evil as well as the good, and perhaps in larger measure. It seems a true statement of these characteristics, true almost to the verge of being a truism, that they are found in the tendency to individualism, which in greater or less measure, has been found in these societies, or in extremest cases, in solitary thinkers who take their stand outside all societies. The right of the individual intellect to be the interpreter of Scripture, instead of accepting an interpretation given as authoritative by Pope, or Council, or Fathers, to go beyond this, and to judge of the evidence on which the authority of Scripture, or any part of Scripture, itself rests, of the grounds on which we believe in the existence of God and of a Divine order resting on His will; this has been the distinguishing feature of the great movement which we recognise by the name of Protestant. If it has been supplemented, as in many cases it has been, by including the work of the Spirit as guiding and illumining the reason, which, left to itself, was admitted to be inadequate to the task of discerning the mysteries of God, it has still been left to the individual intellect to determine how far it possesses that illumination.

It will hardly be questioned here that this emancipation of the minds of men from their long thraldom to an authority which might, at least, be usurped, resting on no legitimate foundation, was an immense step forward in the right direction. It was to theology what the recognition of the rights of the people was in the political history of the time. It stirred men to activity of thought and earnest enquiry instead of a blind acquiescence in the order which they found existing, or in the traditions which they had inherited from their fathers. It impressed them with the sense of a new responsibility as seekers after truth. If it brought new problems and doubts and difficulties before their minds, it gave them at the same time courage to face those difficulties, and led them into the right path of investigation in the hope of a solution. It recognised that God reveals Himself to man through Reason, and Conscience, and Experience, no less really, though it might be less fully, than through Scripture and the Church, and taught men that the knowledge gained by that first Revelation was the test by which they were to judge of the meaning and credentials of the second. Even those who still urged the claims of authority as against the endless variations of private judgment felt the power of the movement, and were compelled to give a new character to their arguments. Every plea for the infallible authority of Pope, or Church, or Scripture had to be submitted to the Reason which men were seeking to persuade to acknowledge its own impotence. Its freedom was recognised up to the point when, in one supreme exercise of volition, it was to determine that it would be no longer free, and would thenceforth submit its judgment to the self-imposed power of the tribunal which it had learnt to look upon as final.

We, in this place, shall hardly question that the gain of the movement which was thus characterised has more than balanced any incidental loss. Even if it had been otherwise, if the loss of unity, of peace, of the sense of certainty had been greater than it has been, it would still remain true that freedom is a nobler state than bondage, that there is a truer unity than that which rests on absolute uniformity in creed, that it is wrong, and not right, for the individual soul to disinherit itself of the gifts which it has received from God in order to avoid the responsibilities which those gifts bring with them. But the test "By their fruits ye shall know them" may be challenged without fear, as applicable not less to systems of thought and methods of enquiry than it is to individual teachers. The whole body of Apologetic literature in which the last three centuries have been fruitful beyond all comparison with any past period of the history of Christendom, and which has never been richer and more effective than in our time, what is it but the outcome of this recognition of what has been rightly called the "verifying faculty¹"

[1] I borrow the phrase from Dr Rowland Williams's paper on *Bunsen's Biblical Researches* in *Essays and Reviews* (p. 83). It was much attacked at the time by those who were alarmed at the tendency of that volume, and Augustine's maxim "*Ne corrigat aeger medicamenta sua*" was quoted against it. But it will be admitted that even the sick man chooses his physician according to the best evidence he can obtain, and that if he has not before him the prescription for his own individual case, but an unclassified Pharmacopœia, he must exercise his discernment in deciding what *medicamenta* are suitable for his own maladies or those of others.

within us, of Reason as the lamp which God has kindled in each man's soul, in order that by following its light, and living by it, we might attain to the perception of the higher light which He has manifested in Christ. If it had been from the first, the duty of a Christian to give to every man who asked him a "reason of the hope" that was in him[1], "an answer with meekness and fear,"— a duty which implied the right of the questioner to ask that reason,—we may say without boasting overmuch, that, at least on the intellectual side of the argument as distinct from the living personal experience, which translates arguments into realities and confirms outward evidence by that of the spirit within us, no age has been so well furnished as our own, with weapons, offensive and defensive, from the armoury of God; that it is an inestimable gain, both as regards the attainment of truth and the maintenance of peace and goodwill in human societies, to have substituted these weapons for those of

[1] 1 Pet. iii. 15.

the older warfare, for the rack, the scaffold and the stake, or, where men did not dare to venture on these, for political and social disqualifications.

Still greater, if possible, is the debt which we owe to the essential principle of Protestantism in its work on the interpretation of the writings whose claim to be the Oracles of God has thus been vindicated. In proportion as it has been true to itself, men have entered the house of the interpreter, and have passed through its richly garnished chambers and have brought out from its treasures things new and old, as well instructed scribes. It is not too much to say that under this method, we have made discoveries in the region of sacred literature no less than in that of natural science. Scripture has been seen to be a library and not a book[1]; each volume in that library has been studied,

---

[1] The idea was indeed latent in the old title of the Vulgate, *Biblia Sacra*, the plural noun which came in mediæval Latinity to be taken as a feminine singular, and was expressed by the term *Bibliotheca*, which Jerome himself applied to it, and which was freely used by writers of the Anglo-Saxon Church.

as other books are studied, as having a history and meaning of its own, fashioned by the mind of the writer, and the environment in the midst of which he lived, and the teaching which he had received from God. Each sentence in every book has received a new meaning, because it has been no longer treated as one of a great collection of texts to be used in controversy, or as rules of life, but as part of an organic whole. The application of the results of the accurate study of language, of history, of character, of psychology, has thrown light upon much that before was dark, and it is almost a truism to say that the life and words of Christ or of St Paul, of Abraham or David or Isaiah, have been brought before men in this age of ours with a clearness and vividness which were unknown to our fathers. You in this University may well count it as one of your special titles to the reverence of the English people that you, in the nineteenth century as in the seventeenth, have been foremost in this work, that you can claim as your children, not a few of the most eminent of those who have acted on the principle of Protestantism in the temper of Catholicity, among whom I may perhaps venture to-day to recognise as one of the noblest of that goodly company, not of the 'chief thirty' only, but of the 'first three,' the teacher whose loss you will soon deplore, while the Church at large welcomes his entry on a new region of activity for his well trained powers[1].

Evil has, however, it cannot be denied, been mingled with the good. This assertion of individualism, of the right of private

[1] This sermon was preached on the Sunday after Dr Lightfoot had been designated as Bishop Baring's successor in the See of Durham. One who belongs to the sister University may freely recognise, without detracting from its special merits, the work which Cambridge has done from the sixteenth century downwards in the criticism and interpretation of Scripture. The list is a long one, and it will be sufficient to name among those belonging to the past, Cranmer, Ridley, Latimer, Rogers (the translator of the Bible), Davenant, Fulke, the elder Lightfoot, Poole (of the *Critici Sacri* and *Synopsis*), Walton (of the Polyglot Bible), Bishop Marsh; and of those who come within our own times, Alford, and Wordsworth, and Trench, and Ellicott, and Maurice (though here Oxford may claim a share), and Scrivener, and Perowne, and Farrar, and Howson, and Cook, and Lightfoot, and Hort, and Westcott.

judgment as such, as distinct from its recognition as a duty, for which we need, as for other duties, a special preparation, and which brings with it very solemn responsibilities, has had in the region of man's religious life, somewhat of the same disintegrating effect as the assertion of the abstract rights of men has had in political society. The right so asserted has been exercised in the spirit of self-will, without the deference which is due, in this, as in all regions of inquiry, from those who do not think and study to those who do, from the scholars of the lowest form to the masters of those who know, from the solitary dreamer to the *consensus* of those who look before and after. Men have claimed a direct illumination, as giving them not only a sufficient light by which to live, and so leading them to holiness, but as enabling them to understand all mysteries and all knowledge. They have inverted Augustine's ingenuous confession, *Errare possum; hæreticus esse nolo*, and taking for granted that they could not err, they have assumed a position of aloofness from the Church which marked them out, as in the true sense of the word, heretical. The results of this spirit are seen, I need not say, in the history of those variations over which Romish controversialists have raised their song of triumph—in schisms and disputes about the infinitely little, which should lie below man's care, or the infinitely great, which lies above his ken—in the loss of all, or nearly all, sense that Christ came not only to redeem this soul and that from the penalty of sin, but to gather the souls so redeemed into a great society with a corporate and perpetual life, with memories stretching back into the past, and hopes reaching forward to the future. The "dissidence of Dissent[1]" has taken in men's thoughts the place of the Communion of Saints, and the one question which each one has been taught to ask himself has been "Am *I* saved from ever-

---

[1] The characteristic watchword, for many years, of the *Nonconformist* newspaper. It has now, however, been withdrawn. *Gutta cavat lapidem*, and the *sæpe cadendo* of Mr Matthew Arnold's gentle iteration would seem to have achieved its victory.

lasting torments" rather than "am I living as a child of the Kingdom, a citizen of the heavenly City?"

Not seldom, also, in the history of Protestantism, has it proved untrue to itself. It had rejected the authority of an infallible Pope or an infallible Church, but the spirit which it had cast out returned, and instead of believing, in the quietness and confidence of faith, that the Word of God would prove itself to be true to those who tried it rightly, it assumed that the books that contained that Word were infallible in all things. It condemned in advance, as impious and unbelieving, all conclusions in history or science which seemed at variance with any part of its teaching—all expansions in doctrine, or discipline or ritual which could not be found in some definite form within its pages. Lavishing what Hooker has well called "incredible praises"[1] on Holy

[1] Hooker, *Eccl. Polity*, II. VIII. 7. "And as incredible praises given unto men do often abate and impair the credit of their deserved commendation; so we must likewise take great heed, lest in attributing unto Scripture more than it can have, the incredibility of that do cause even those things which indeed it hath most abundantly, to be less generally esteemed.

Scripture, they turned it into an idol to which they paid a blind and unreasoning homage, ascribing to it a character which it does not claim for itself, and using it for purposes for which it was not needed, for which also its very form or fashion might have shewn that it was never intended.

The history of the relations between the Church of England and these latter aspects of Protestantism has not been a very happy or creditable history. We cannot study the bearing of the great Puritan party, to which we may look as the parent of all later forms of Dissent, without seeing that there were in it many elements of nobleness. Its very name—in itself a far grander name than Protestant—bore its witness, though given, it might be, in derision, of a high ideal of purity in doctrine, in worship and in morals[1]. The

[1] It would be interesting here also, as in the case of Protestant, to trace the *genesis* of the name, who first used it, when it first appeared, and the like. Historians, however, even Neal, are vague on these points, and we learn little more than that the party that desired a further reformation of the doctrine, discipline, and ritual, of the Church of England, began about A.D. 1564 to be known as Puritans. In Shake-

men who were so described were marked by an intensity of faith which has seldom been seen working on so large a scale since the first ages of the Church. Sin and holiness, and pardon and peace, and heaven and hell, were to them intense realities. They were as the salt of the nation, preserving it from the putrescence with which it was threatened by the revived paganism and sensualism of the Renaissance. They fought for the civil as well as the religious liberties of Englishmen against a tyranny that was at once ecclesiastical and Erastian[1]. Even their Sab-

---

speare's *Twelfth Night* (written between 1590-1602) in which Malvolio is described as "a kind of Puritan" (Act II. 3), it appears as a current-term of reproach. The title-page of a *Life of Joseph Alleyne* by C. Stanford (1873) gives, as a quotation from Erasmus, the words: *Sit anima mea cum Puritanis Anglicanis.* No reference is given, and I have been unable to verify the passage. Assuming its genuineness it would seem to imply that the term had been applied, perhaps, even then, with something of a sneer, to the Oxford Reformers, and that More and Colet were the first bearers of the name.

[1] It will hardly be contended, even by the warmest admirers of the Anglican party under the Stuart regime, that the Starchamber and High Commission Courts, dominant as was Laud's influence in them, were true Church tribunals in their constitution. Even "His Majesty's Declaration" pre-

batarianism, overstrained and Judaising as it was, stands out in honourable contrast with the coarse comedies and the brutal bear-baitings which were then the recognised recreation of an English Sunday. But with this there was all the narrowness that grows out of ignorance and panic. They sought to obliterate all traces of the continuity of the Church's life, and took fright at things that were absolutely indifferent because they had belonged to its pre-reformation period[1]. They acted too often in the very spirit of

fixed to the Thirty-nine Articles, though interesting as the first example of a 'Broad Church' comprehensiveness in the interpretation of dogmatic formulæ, assumes, in "prohibiting the least difference from the said Articles, not suffering unnecessary disputations, altercations, or questions to be raised," and decreeing that "all further curious search be laid aside," an authority more in harmony with the theory of the Swiss physician whom we know as Erastus (Thomas Liebler, of the Swiss Baden) than with either the Episcopal or Presbyterian 'platform' of Church polity.

[1] The vestments, the surplice, the sign of the cross, the position of the Lord's Table, the use of chanting and instrumental music, the ring in marriage, were among the most prominent of the *adiaphora*, round which the battle of controversy raged in the sixteenth and seventeenth centuries. Here, too, it would seem that the prejudices and passions of the past have a potent vitality.

sectarianism. When they had their brief hour of triumph, they used it without pity, and shewed that the spirit of intolerance survived even in the champions of freedom. And the rulers of the Church on the other hand—Can we hold them blameless? Where it would have been their wisdom to conciliate the prejudices of the weak, and to utilise the reserve force of spiritual energies, and to concede a little for the sake of gaining much, we find them bent on a froward retention of customs and formulæ which had not even the prestige of antiquity—insisting on a rigorous uniformity and enforcing it by severest penalties. Both sides alike act and speak as though they had never heard the words "We that are strong ought to bear the infirmities of the weak, and not to please ourselves[1]." If we

[1] The oppressive measures recorded in Walker's "Sufferings of the Clergy," the expulsion of many hundreds of that order from their cures and homes under the Long Parliament and Cromwell must be borne in mind when we censure, as we are compelled to censure, the over-bearing harshness which was shewn at the Savoy Conference, and which issued in the "black Bartholomew" fixed by the Act of Uniformity of 1662, for the deprivation of the 2000 Presbyterian Minis-

may believe of many on both sides that they were casting out devils in the name of Christ, even though they followed not with those whom we follow, we must fear that many also came under the condemnation passed on those who do not gather, and are therefore as he that scattereth abroad. Golden opportunities were wasted of which we cannot hope that their like will ever again be given to us, and we are compelled to look the *fait accompli* in the face, and to acknowledge that the sentence 'Too late' is written on all schemes for the union and reconciliation of the dissenting communities which we see around us, with each other or with the Church.

But accepting, as we must, that lamentable ters, many of whom were as the salt of the earth in the holiness of their lives, and most of whom were yearning for Communion with the Established Church, if but a few concessions had been made to them in things indifferent. A few leading minds like Stillingfleet, Tillotson, Burnet, Crofts, Baxter, sought in the forty years that followed, for terms of comprehension, and the Revolution of 1688 seemed at one time to hold out a hope that the contending parties might be drawn together by the sense of a common danger. On the Country party in the House of Commons, the country Clergy in the Lower House of Convocation, rests the responsibility of having frustrated all such well-intentioned efforts.

heritage, are we simply to content ourselves with the proverb of despair and to let the children's teeth be set on edge for ever by the sour grapes of which the fathers have eaten? Are we still to look on those who are our bone and our flesh, who have fought the same battles against the same foes, with a supercilious and discourteous scorn[1]? Are we to condemn as schismatics those who have been alienated from us at least as much by the frowardness of our fathers, as by the perverseness of theirs? Are we to confine our sympathies and efforts at re-union to the far-off Churches of the East, or the corrupt communion of the Latin Church, while we shrink from contact and co-operation with the more energetic and evangelic life of the Reformed Churches of Western Europe, or with the communities to which it would be hard, on any New Testament principles, to deny the name of Churches, that exist among our-

[1] The existence of this feeling as dominant in the upper classes of English Society in the past, and not extinct in the present, will, I suppose, hardly be questioned. It shews itself even now in the most opposite quarters, in the Bishop

selves[1]? We as Churchmen need not shrink from following Cosin[2] in holding communion with "the Protestant and best Reformed Churches" of France and Germany and recognising the validity of their ordinations, in declaring that "in what part of the world so

of Lincoln and Mr Matthew Arnold, as a survival of the old leaven. When we sneer at Dissenters as "Philistines," or deny to their teachers the conventional title of respect which indicates nothing more than that they are recognised by the body to which they belong, as qualified instructors, we are reproducing the old arrogance and the old bitterness of our fathers.

[1] It will be acknowledged that the Non-conformist Societies are congregations of baptised persons, confessing the name of Christ, taking scripture as their rule of faith. It would be hard to prove that St Paul would not have recognised such a congregation as an *Ecclesia*, though he might have deplored, as we deplore, the imperfect knowledge, or the inherited conviction, which separates them from communion with the wider *Ecclesia* of the nation.

[2] The extract that follows is from Cosin's Will (*Works* in *Anglo-Catholic Library*, I. p. XXXII.) After his expulsion from the Mastership of Peterhouse, he took refuge in France and lived at Charenton, not far from Paris. He communicated with the Protestant (more strictly, of course, we should say, the *Reformed*) Churches there, and they allowed him to officiate in their congregations, using the Liturgy of the Church of England. When consulted as to the lawfulness of such communion he wrote, "To speak my mind freely to you I would not wish any of ours absolutely to refuse communicating in their Church, or determine it to be unlawful, for fear of a greater scandal that may thereupon arise, than we can tell how to answer or excuse." Ibid. p. XXX.

ever any Churches are extant, bearing the name of Christ and professing the true Catholic Faith, and worshipping and calling upon God the Father, the Son, and Holy Ghost, with one heart and voice, if anywhere we be now hindered actually to be joined with them, either by distance of countries or variance amongst men or by any hindrance whatsoever, yet always in our mind and affection we should join and unite with them." We may well be content to walk in the steps of Sancroft in urging on the Clergy " that they have a very tender regard to our brethren, the Protestant Dissenters . . . persuading them, if it may be, to a full compliance with our Church, or, at least, that 'whereto we have already attained, we may all walk by the same rule, and mind the same thing;' praying for the universal blessed union of all Reformed Churches, both at home and abroad, against our common enemies[1]." We may acknowledge with thankfulness that many steps have been taken to the right application *in*

[1] D'Oyly, *Life of Sancroft*, p. 196.

*meliorem partem,* of the "cross clauses of the league of Christians." One by one the statutes which embodied the vindictive intolerance of the seventeenth century have been swept away. The operation of the Conscience Clause in our National Schools no longer throws us into an hysterical alarm. The admission of Dissenters to our Colleges no longer rouses the fierce passions of controversy, as it did when the Master mind of this your University was forced to resign his tutorship because he pleaded for the cause of justice and of charity[1]. Bishops and Professors of the Church are seen working side by side with Nonconformist scholars in the great task of translating and interpreting the sacred books which are the common heritage of all. They have recognised that it was right to inaugurate that work by participation in the act which witnesses of a higher unity

[1] I refer, of course, in this to Bishop Thirlwall's pamphlet on the Admission of Dissenters, and the proceedings that followed on it. (See *Edinburgh Review*, Vol. CXLIII). For the now almost forgotten controversy of the Conscience Clauses I may refer to the Bishop's Charge for 1866, in the second volume of Dean Perowne's Edition of his *Remains*.

## Protestantism. 75

than that which is limited by outward uniformity in dogma or in ritual—that the true Elevation of the Host was that which raised it above our manifold divisions[1]. It remains

[1] I owe the expression and the thought to the late F. D. Maurice. It may freely be admitted that the Communions in Westminster Abbey, in June 1870, to which all members of the two Revision Companies were invited, bore an entirely exceptional character, and that the Rubric which directs that none should be admitted to communion but "such persons as have been confirmed, or are ready and desirous to be confirmed" was, *pro hac vice*, disregarded. But the rubric itself is, on the other hand, a dead letter in its prohibitive, though happily a living ordinance in its directive, aspects. The English Church has never adopted the Scotch plan of "fencing" the Lord's Table, and in the public administration of Holy Communion, we, for the most part, are entirely ignorant whether the condition has been complied with, or whether those who present themselves for Communicants have previously been trained in her Communion. We take for granted that they are "worthy" because they seek for fellowship with Christ and His Church in His ordinance, that their consciences find nothing in our Order for Holy Communion to repel them from it. On this occasion men were on the point of starting on a great work which was planned for the good of English-speaking Christendom. Both Houses of Convocation had deliberately invited Nonconformist Scholars of many different denominations to take part in that work. Was it supposed that they could not possibly join in prayer for the Divine blessing on their labours, that they were to be students of the Divine Book with no sense of a Divine unity binding them together? And if they could thus draw near to the Father through the Son, was there not a cause for suspending, for the time, the restrictions

for you, who are rising to take your place in the ranks of the clergy or laity of the Church of England, to carry on the good work to its completeness; to meet any grievances that yet remain in the temper, not of a jealous exclusiveness, but of an equitable charity[1];

[1] which excluded them from the highest Act of that access? Did not each Communicant, with whatever sacramental theories he might approach the Table, confess that there was in that Memorial Feast something which was wider than all theories, and that there was nothing in the liturgy in which he joined, though there might be that in it which he would wish otherwise, to hinder his participation in it? Was it not wise and charitable to leave it to the conscience of each to say whether he could make that confession?

[1] I have no wish to enter here into a discussion of the vexed question of which we see the outcome in the endless Dissenters' Burials Bills of the last few years; but no language can well be too strong in deprecation of the tone and temper in which that discussion is commonly approached by those who claim to represent Church interests in Parliament or the press. There is the old bearing of the Cavaliers to the Roundheads, of the Country party of the Restoration to the Presbyterian. There are the old cries of the "Church in danger" and "the thin end of the wedge," the old incapacity to enter into the feelings of those from whom we differ, and to understand that a grievance may be very real even though it be only "sentimental," the old *Non possumus* of an irrational resistance. The history of the Conscience Clause is not in this matter without its lessons. Men nail their colours to the mast and raise the cry of "no surrender." At last a change comes, more thorough and sweeping than that which they had resisted, and they find that what they dreaded

to recognise that those who are not against us in the great battle against ignorance and evil are on our side—and so to inherit the blessing which belongs to "the repairers of the breach and the restorers of paths to dwell in." (Isai. lviii. 12.)

takes its place in the normal order of the nation's life, without the convulsive and catastrophic changes which their fears had prognosticated.

## III.  AGNOSTICISM.

Acts xvii. 23.

*I found an altar with this inscription,* TO THE UNKNOWN GOD.

Rom. i. 19.

*That which may be known of God is manifest in them.*

We can, without much difficulty or risk of error, picture to ourselves the thoughts and feelings of the Apostle as he walked through the streets of Athens, or stood talking to such as would listen to him in its *agora*. The stately temples that move the world's wonder, the statues of Athene, or Poseidon, or Apollo in every courtyard, the Hermes busts at the corner of every street, these were for him not, as they have been to many, a "thing of beauty, and a joy for ever," but the witness of a fatal degradation. He had seen many Greek cities—Tarsus, Antioch, Lystra,—but none had so stirred his spirit into a paroxysm of indignant grief. That feeling was but intensified by the fact that the Wisdom no less than the Art of the Greek world was here presented to his mind in its highest and most perfect form. Those brave words of Epicureans and Stoics as to the Supreme Good and the chief end of life, that supercilious disdain of the popular worship which the philosopher knew to be radically wrong, yet had not courage to abandon, that high ideal of conformity to the Eternal Order on the one hand, or of a serene equilibrium and maximum of enjoyment on the other—what had they done to raise the mass of mankind to clearer thoughts of God, or greater purity of life?

His eye had, however, rested on words which seemed to him of profound significance, and gave a new direction to his thoughts. We need not now discuss what was the meaning of the words TO THE UNKNOWN GOD, to him who had dedicated the altar. Was it the extreme result of Polytheism, unable to identify its benefactor among the gods many and lords many of Greek mythology, and thinking of one more to be added to the list who as yet was without a name? Was it, as seems more probable, like the SIGNUM INDEPREHENSIBILIS DEI on the Mithraic group from Ostia[1], the utterance of a yearning cry

[1] The inscription may be found in Orelli, II. p. 1000; the altar on which it appears is in the Vatican Museum. It represents, like most of those dedicated to the worship of Mithras, a youthful figure sacrificing a bull. The inscription runs:

SIGNUM INDEPREHENSIBILIS DEI
G. VALERIUS HERCULES. SACERDOS.
P. P.

De Rossi thinks that it belongs to the last half of the third century, when the worship of Mithras (of which the continued observance of the *Dies Solis* is perhaps a survival) came to be fashionable as a rival to the claims of that of Christ. It had, however, been introduced at Ostia as far back as the time of Pompeius (Plutarch, *Pomp.*), and Tertullian (*De Præscr.* c. XL.) bears witness to its wide-spread prevalence in his own time, and speaks of it as presenting many points of resemblance to the *cultus* of Christians. There is, therefore, no anachronism in supposing that an altar of this type may have existed in Athens in the first century. It may be added that the absence of any reference to such an inscription in Greek writers is against the assumption of a much earlier date."

for the Undiscovered One, Supreme above all Gods—worshipped in many lands and under many names—but as yet revealed to none, and wrapt in the impenetrable darkness of an eternal mystery? The latter was, at all events, the interpretation which the Apostle put upon the words when he made it the text of that memorable discourse before the court, or within the precincts, of the Areopagus. I dare not venture now, great as the temptation is, to follow that discourse step by step, and to trace its bearing on those who listened, the devout worshippers—the gossiping idlers—the philosophic disputants. It will be enough to note that he sees in the inscription a token of that awe of the unseen and unknown forces that lie round us, which is at once the germ of all true religion, and the source of the basest superstitions; that in contrast with the false idea of God of which the latter were developments, he proclaims the true philosophy of worship, almost, as far as its negative aspect is concerned, in the very words of

Lucretius[1], as resting on the thought that God needs nothing at our hands, but gives all things; that he adds to this the outline of a new philosophy of History as being, in all its complexity, in "the times before appointed, and the bounds of men's habitations," the school in which God educates mankind, waking longings which remain unsatisfied, leading them through devious ways, as men feeling their way and groping in the twilight dusk, after the Eternal and Invisible. To that outward witness there is, he adds, an answering voice within us. The Stoics were right in their belief that every man is a Temple to himself, and that in that temple he may find God. "He is not far from every one of us." More truly than in the witness of creation, than in the records of experience,

---

[1] Lucret. *De Nat. Rer.* II. 645—650:
"Omnis enim per se divôm natura necesse est
  Immortali aevo summa cum pace fruatur,
  Semota ab nostris rebus sejunctaque longe;
  Nam privata dolore omni, privata periclis,
  Ipsa suis pollens opibus, nil indiga nostri,
  Nec bene promeritis capitur, neque tangitur ira."
Acts xvii. 25 "Neither is worshipped with men's hands, as though He needed anything."

he may find in the depths of consciousness, in the law written in his heart, in the thoughts that accuse each other, the token that every child of man is a child of God. "We also are His offspring[1]."

The speech came to an end, but not so the train of thought of which it was, as it were, the firstfruits. The Apostle's mind worked on in that groove, and sought to solve the problems which had thus presented themselves. How was it that, though God had not left Himself without witness, giving showers from heaven

---

[1] Dr Lightfoot has given some striking illustrations in his Excursus on *St Paul and Seneca* (*Philippians*, p. 288):

"Temples are not to be built to God of stones piled on high: He must be consecrated in the heart of each man" (*Fragm.* 123)..."God is near thee; He is with thee: He is within" (*Ep. Mor.* XLI. 1)..."Thou shalt not form Him of silver or gold. A true likeness of God cannot be moulded of this material" (*Ep. Mor.* XXXI.).

Another may be given from a contemporary poet, the nephew of Seneca and the namesake of the writer of the Acts:

" Estne dei sedes nisi terra, et pontus et aer,
  Et coelum et virtus? Superos quid petimus ultra?
  Jupiter est quodcumque vides, quocunque moveris."
                Lucan, *Phars.* IX. 578—580.

Many other illustrations will, of course, be found in most Commentaries on the Acts.

and fruitful seasons, filling men's hearts with food and gladness[1], men either shewed by their worship, as in the popular ritual, that they knew Him not, even by the hearing of the ear, or as in the altar to the Unknown God, confessed their ignorance? What adequate explanation could be given of those times of ignorance during which God had overlooked, and, as it were, connived at the world's evils, tolerating the sins of men, while as yet there were no signs of the repentance which is the one condition of forgiveness? If the history of the world was the education of mankind, what was the goal to which that education was directed?

The whole argument of the Epistle to the Romans is the outcome of the thoughts which were working in St Paul's mind in that speech at Athens. It is not reading too much between the lines to find in the very words which open the argument an echo of the inscription which had been the origin of those thoughts. The despairing confession

[1] Acts xiv. 17.

of the altar to the Unknown and Unknowable God is met by the assertion that "That which may be known, the knowable, of God is manifest in them[1]," that the ignorance into which men have fallen is the result wrought out by their unwillingness to face the thought of God—that this led, in its turn, to a baser view of their own nature and of the end of life[2]. As in the entail of curses on which the Greek poets loved to dwell, one sin became the parent of another, which was at once its natural consequence and its divinely ordained penalty[3]. With unshrinking hand he tears aside the veil of a flimsy optimism which boasted of the triumphs of wisdom and art, and culture, and in words that make us shudder, lays bear the putrid and leprous cancers

---

[1] ʼΑγνώστῳ Θεῷ, Acts xvii. 23. Τὸ γνωστὸν τοῦ Θεοῦ, Rom. i. 19.
[2] Rom. i. 21—32.
[3] Æsch. *Agam.* 757,
τὸ γὰρ δυσσεβὲς ἔργον
μέτα μὲν πλείονα τίκτει, σφετέρᾳ δ' εἰκότα γέννᾳ.
\* \* \* \* \* \*
φιλεῖ δὲ τίκτειν Ὕβρις μὲν παλαιὰ νεά-
ζουσαν ἐν κακοῖς βροτῶν Ὕβριν.

that were eating into the life of the Greek and Roman world and plunging it into a fathomless corruption.

That dark and terrible picture might well have crushed out all hope. No older Manichean, no modern Pessimist, could have constructed, it might have seemed, a stronger indictment against the divine attributes of wisdom, and love, and power. Did not the history of the world seem a colossal failure, the education of mankind one that ended in ever-deepening ignorance and guilt? St Paul could not rest in that thought any more than he could satisfy his questioning intellect with the phrases of a Stoic apathy or Epicurean tranquillity. He found what helped to sustain him and give him guidance in the record of another failure that more nearly concerned himself and the race of which he was a member. Israel had not been left to the twofold witness of creation and of conscience, but had been chosen for a higher knowledge and a special revelation. Law and Psalm and Ritual and Prophecy had preserved them from the darkness that had brooded over the heathen. Were they after all better than the heathen? Had they been truer to the Law written on the Tables of Stone than the Gentiles had been to the law written in their hearts? The answer to those questions was a sad stern negative. Both Jew and Gentile had alike come short of the glory of God— were alike guilty before Him—shut up under sin and condemnation. Each had had sufficient knowledge to be "without excuse;" neither had so used his knowledge as to attain to holiness and peace[1]. The darkness on this view might have seemed blacker and more abysmal than before. If Israel was rejected, with all its special prerogatives as a chosen and peculiar people, what hope was there for the Gentile world? It was given to St Paul to see the gleams of a Divine light breaking through the darkness. We cannot say that he solves the whole problem, and

[1] Comp. the whole argument of Rom. i. 18—iii. 19. We note the terrible reiteration of the ἀναπολόγητος in Rom. i. 20, ii. 1, as addressed alike to idolater, philosopher, and Jew.

removes all difficulties. The varying interpretations that have been put upon his words hinder us from saying that his Theodicy, his vindication of the ways of God, is speculatively complete[1]. He himself is the first to confess that those ways are "past finding out." But he has seen, at least, what we may call the drift of things—the purpose which is working out a result for good and not for evil. Men had been led—and were being led—

[1] It will hardly be questioned that logically the argument falls short of completeness, unless we carry on the train of thought of Rom. v. and xi. to the conclusions adopted by Origen and later teachers, who have cherished the wider hope of a universal restoration. The "much more" of Rom. v. 18—20 is hardly satisfied by the "salvation" of a predestined few out of the millions of mankind. When we read that "all Israel shall be saved" (Rom. xi. 26), the words suggest something more than the perdition of a hundred generations and the pardon of a remnant of the hundred and first. And yet it is clear that the Apostle shrinks, as most of the Masters of those who know have shrunk, from dogmatically affirming that universal restoration. He is content to rest in the belief that that is God's purpose, that He is leading men through ways that baffle our investigation to that far-off result, but he cannot exclude the thought that it is possible that the fatal gift of freedom which frustrates the loving purpose of God now on earth may frustrate it for ever. It is not without significance that Rom. xi. should have been the favourite chapter alike of ultra-Calvinists and of Thomas Erskine of Linlathen.

Jew and Gentile alike, by a terrible experience to feel their impotence apart from God, to welcome the revelation of God in Christ by which they have access to the Father. The mercies of God were manifested even in the sentence of condemnation. He had concluded all in unbelief that He might have pity upon all[1].

I have dwelt at this length on the main line of St Paul's treatment of this great question—the ever-recurring question which has haunted the souls of men in the former times as well as in the latter—because I am persuaded that it is on these lines of thought that we must travel if we would meet, with any adequacy, the special forms of scepticism or unbelief that seem to us characteristic of our own time. Those forms present, it is obvious, many features analogous to those with which he had to deal. It seems a strange outcome of the eighteen centuries which have passed since he thus thought and spoke, that men should still be thinking of God as the

[1] Rom. xi. 32.

Unknown and the Unknowable—yet so we know it is[1]. The prophets of Science tell us that we can know the phenomena of the universe, but that we cannot know their cause, and that it is our wisdom to keep within the limits of the knowable. The prophets of culture, with the savour of an earlier and better training still lingering in their souls, go a step beyond this, and tell us not untruly, however incompletely, that there are signs all around us and within us of "a power not ourselves, a stream of tendency, that makes for righteousness[2]," and that therefore it is our

---

[1] Huxley's *Lay Sermons*, p. 20, "The theology of the present has become more scientific than that of the past, because it has not only renounced idols of wood and idols of stone, but begins to see the necessity of breaking in pieces the idols built up of books and traditions and fine-spun ecclesiastical cobwebs, and of cherishing the noblest and most human of man's emotions by worship, 'for the most part of the silent sort,' at the altar of the Unknown and Unknowable."

[2] Matthew Arnold, *Literature and Dogma*, p. 41. "For Science God is simply the stream of tendency by which all things fulfil the law of their being." One cannot read this and other writings of Mr Arnold's without hearing in them the two voices whose dissonant notes have not yet been brought into accord. On the one hand there is a manifest capacity for almost mystical emotion. He sympathises with, and half shares, the love which Israel felt for the Eternal,

wisdom to be righteous—that this is all that we can know of what we call God, and that when we ascribe to Him a Will, and Purpose and Character, still more when we venture to interpret His dealings with mankind or to accept a revelation from Him, we are simply falling back into the anthropomorphic conceptions which have been the source of all

the Father. He confesses truly enough that the "Power in us and around us is best described by the name of this authoritative, but yet tender and protecting relation" (p. 35), that "the more we experience its shelter, the more we feel that it is protecting even to tenderness" (p. 65). On the other he is repelled by the introduction of a scholastic term like "personality" into popular rhetoric, and by what seem to him platform phrases about "a moral and intelligent Governor of the Universe" (p. 26), and will not ask himself whether these phrases are not after all identical in meaning with those which he adopts himself. Is there, we may ask, any great gulf of thought between a "Power not ourselves that makes for righteousness" and "a moral Governor of the Universe"? Are we thinking of God only as "a magnified and non-natural man," because we ascribe to Him a Wisdom and Love and Righteousness, the ideas of which have been gathered indeed from our own conscious experience, but which we recognise as being free in Him from the imperfections that cloud all manifestations of them which we have seen in men? In his protests against the "insane license of affirmation" which characterises our theological systems, most controversialists will recognise a rebuke deserved by their opponents, most impartial students of controversy a warning by which all may profit.

perversions and falsehoods, in the religious history of mankind. The prophets of art follow up the lesson by proclaiming that its province and that of ethics are unconnected with each other—and that the end of the former is but to depict faithfully whatever it finds to its hand that may minister to our sense of beauty and bring about a maximum of enjoyment. The more sensuous, realistic forms of art, in poetry, and painting, and sculpture, fulfil this purpose more than the ideal, or mystic, or ascetic forms that presuppose a standard of holiness, and those who follow them are therefore truer to their vocation. All alike take up their taunting proverb against what seems to them the shadowy projection of our hopes and fears into the dim future that lies beyond the veil. Epicureans and Stoics may listen to the preacher as he speaks in their own terms, of righteousness and temperance, but when he proclaims a judgment to come and tells them that God has appointed Jesus who was crucified to be Judge of quick and dead, the result is now as it was of old. Some mock, in various tones of brutal or refined derision. Some, let us hope, there may be, who will say "We will hear thee again of this matter."

What kind of worship, in act or word, is to be the expression of the thoughts of those who, while they undermine the groundwork of all devotion, still recognise the religious instincts of mankind, as an essential element of their nature, that must have a legitimate outflow, or, at least, a safety valve, lest they should explode and shatter the edifice of theory, it is not easy to say. The worship to be paid at the altar of the Unknown and Unknowable is, we are told, to be "for the most part of the silent sort," and it must be admitted that it would be a hard task to construct a liturgy on the basis of an absolute nescience of Him whom we ignorantly worship. The worship of humanity, of its saints and heroes as having an immortality in the memory of mankind, and the after harvest of the seeds which they have sown, may end, as it seems likely to end, in an unlimited apotheosis of the discoverers and benefactors of the race, but of each god so created it will be true that he is shadowy, impersonal, unsubstantial, and that after all prayer and praise, there will be neither voice nor answer nor any that regardeth[1]. The Christian of the nineteenth century will find it as hard to turn from the worship of a personal Father to that of an impersonal "drift of things" as the Athenian did to think of a Vortex as seated

---

[1] What we may call the positive, or constructive, side of Positivism has been described by Mr Huxley as "Catholicism *minus* Christianity." It meets man's cravings for a *cultus* of some kind, with a calendar of heroes and saints and sages almost as multitudinous as that of the Church of Rome, with a hierarchy whose ideal task is to dominate, as she has done, over the intellect and will of men. It has been easier, however, for those who call themselves disciples of Comte to follow him in the task of pulling down than of building up; and while thousands take up the phrases that shut out the question, Can we know God? as belonging only to the first stage of human progress, the priests and the worshippers of the "religion of humanity" may be counted on one's fingers. And yet it has been said with truth that the thoughts which underlie that religion are not the weakest, but the noblest elements in Comte's teaching, are "not only reconcileable with Christianity, but are essentially Christian." The Positivist theory "so far from advancing anything novel in such teaching, simply places us once again in the original Christian point of view of the Cosmos" (Westcott, *Aspects of Positivism in relation to Christianity* in *Contemporary Review*, vol. VIII. p. 383).

on the throne of Zeus[1]. The worship of the beautiful in art is likely to issue, as it did of old, in hymns to Aphrodite and a sensuous ritual of measureless impurities[2]. We turn from these dreams and mirage phantoms of an impossible devotion, as with a sense of relief and reality, to the truer utterances of those who though they confessed that they had not found God were yet in earnest seeking after Him, to the traditional death-prayer which some mediæval sceptic passed upon the world as coming from the lips of Aris-

---

[1] Strepsiades, "ὁρᾷς οὖν, ὡς ἀγαθὸν τὸ μανθάνειν, οὐκ ἔστιν, ὦ Φειδιππίδη, Ζεύς, ἀλλά τις Δῖνος βασιλεύει, τὸν Δί᾽ ἐξεληλακώς."
    Aristoph. *Nub.* 805.

[2] I am not over-conversant with the literature of the higher criticism of art, and do not care to quote illustrative extracts, but the verses and popular essays which meet one in the current journalism of the day tend, it will scarcely be denied, to a glorification,—almost, one might say, an apotheosis,—of Nakedness, which presents but too obvious points of parallelism to the St Simonian "rehabilitation of the flesh." Not once or twice in the history of mankind have we seen the outcome of this gilded putrescence, and have learnt how it eats into a nation's life, and ends as in the poetry of Catullus, the novels of Petronius, and the art of Capreæ. The "Palace of Art" which an earlier generation was taught to admire, had no galleries of lupanarian *tableaux*.

totle, *Causa causarum, miserere mei*[1], to the touching, sad, yet not hopeless, words which we read at Westminster on the tomb of the statesman-poet, and which embody the same prayer addressed to the God whom he knew only as the *Ens Entium,* for in that *Miserere* we read the faith which from the beginning of the world has justified, the sinner's consciousness that he needs forgiveness and that there is One ready to forgive[2].

It is not enough, however, to point out

---

[1] The prayer is referred to by Fiddes in his defence of Sheffield's epitaph (p. 40) as found in Cœlius Rhodigenius (II. 17, § 34), and it runs thus: "*Fœde hanc vitam intravi; anxius vixi; trepidus egredior; Causa Causarum, Miserere mei.*" That writer, however, does not give the words, and I write them from my recollection of an Oxford Lecture by the present Dean of Wells, in 1842.

[2] The whole of this part of the epitaph (on the tomb of Sheffield, Duke of Buckinghamshire) is worth giving:

"Dubius, sed non improbus, vixi;
Incertus morior, non perturbatus.
Humanum est nescire et errare.
   Deo confido
Omnipotenti benevolentissimo:
Ens Entium, miserere mei."

The vacant space in the fourth line was to have been filled up with "Christum adveneror," but this was rejected by Atterbury as not sufficiently orthodox.—Stanley's *Westminster Abbey*, p. 247.

the inadequacy of these substitutes for the faith and the worship of Christendom. We may learn something even from those who appear, as in some sense, its enemies. There is an element of truth in the protests which they utter against the anthropomorphic tendency that shews itself too often in our thoughts of the Divine Nature. While we rightly contend that no conception of that Nature is thinkable which is not moulded in the forms of human thought—that we must take our idea of the righteousness and love of God from what we know of the righteousness and love of Man, and that it introduces an inextricable and intolerable confusion, if we reason, as some of the defenders of our faith have reasoned, as if the two were generically different, so that the one cannot be measured by the standard of the other[1], the history of

---

[1] The argument that we cannot reason from the ideas which we connect with human righteousness, truth, love, wisdom to what would or would not be consistent with those attributes in the Divine Nature, is but too familiar to the student of Calvinistic and other controversies. We find it in its most philosophic form in Dean Mansel's *Bampton Lectures*.

theological speculations, often, alas, of that speculation as translated into action, shews us that men have in too large a measure transferred their own imperfections, their own narrowness and want of love, to Him in whom all is perfect. We cannot ask ourselves what were the thoughts of God underlying the creed of a Philip II. or a Dominic (may we not add, in some measure, of a Tertullian and an Augustine, of a Dante and a Calvin?) without feeling that they were clouding the divine light with their own darkness, making sad the hearts that God had not made sad, that they reasoned, as Caliban may have reasoned out his system of theology as to the nature of his "dam's God Setebos," from what they would have done had they been in the place

We have no "right to assume that there is, if not a perfect identity, at least an exact resemblance between the moral nature of man and that of God; that the laws and principles of infinite justice are but magnified images of those which are manifested on a finite scale" (2nd ed. p. 212). In words which seem almost as if it came from the camp of the enemy and not of an ally, we are told that "we find ourselves baffled in every attempt to conceive an infinite moral nature, or its condition, an infinite personality."

of God[1]; that to the worshipper of the *eidôla* of the Market-place and the Den, no less than to those of the idols of wood or stone, the psalmist's words, spoken as from the mouth of God, were but too justly applicable, "Thou thoughtest that I was altogether such a one as thyself[2]." The true safeguard against an unworthy anthropomorphism is found, not in taking refuge in the thought that God is unknowable and unthinkable, but for those who are without the revelation of God in Christ, in reasoning upwards from all that the *consensus* of mankind has most reverenced

---

[1] Most readers will recognise the reference to Mr Browning's poem, *Caliban upon Setebos*, or *Natural Theology in the Island*, in his *Dramatis Personæ*. As a psychological study the poem stands in manifestly designed correspondence and contrast with the higher form of anthropomorphic thought in the *Death in the Desert* in the same volume. I quote the following from the latter poem.
"Before the point was mooted 'What is God?'
 No savage man inquired 'What am myself?'
 Much less replied 'First, last, and best of things.'
 Man takes that title now, if he believes
 Might can exist with neither will nor love
 In God's case—what he names now 'Nature's Law'—
 While in himself he recognises love
 No less than might or will: and rightly takes."

[2] Ps. l. 21.

and loved in man; for those who walk in the light of that revelation, in looking on the human character of Jesus as the standard by which to measure all our conceptions of the Eternal Will and Purpose. What God is, is made known to us, as far as the Finite can apprehend the Infinite, by what Jesus was. "He that hath seen Him hath seen the Father[1]." In the light of that revelation we need not fear the reproach of holding an anthropomorphic creed. Too often, we may fear, the reproach comes from those who shrink from any distinct thought of the Personality of God, because they shrink from the burden even of their own personal being as being brought face to face with His. It is not without significance that one of the leaders of scientific thought should have hinted at the seeming paradox, that it may be questioned whether "there is anything really anthropomorphic even in man's nature[2]," whe-

[1] John xiv. 9.
[2] Huxley, *Lay Sermons*, p. 180. "As the ages lengthen the borders of Physicism increase. The territories of the bastards are all annexed to Science, and even Theology, in

ther, i. e., all that we think of as most distinctive of man, the thought that looks before and after—the consciousness of sin—the yearning after holiness—the enduring faith of the martyr—the foul crime of the murderer and the adulterer, are not all alike on the same level, as "automatic functions" of the "cunningest of Nature's clocks."

If we ask, as we survey these and other movements of thought around us, as we trace their action on ourselves, in what they have originated, and what constitutes their strength, we shall find, if I mistake not, that they have a twofold birth. There is first, what we may describe, in the language of one who has given to the world his confessions of the way in which they acted on himself, as the Neme-

---

her purer forms, has ceased to be anthropomorphic, however she may talk. Anthropomorphism has taken stand in its last fortress, man himself. But Science closely invests the walls; and Philosophers gird themselves to battle upon the last and greatest of all speculative problems. Does human Nature present any free, volitional, and truly anthropomorphic element, or is it only the cunningest amongst all Nature's clocks? Some, among whom I count myself, think that the battle will for ever remain a drawn one."

sis of Faith[1]. The blind acceptance of dogmas that rested only on human authority, that had never been tested by, and could not bear the test of, Scripture, of Reason and of Conscience, has been followed by a natural reaction. The imperious command "Believe all that the Church tells you to believe, or believe nothing," has led sometimes, as we see in the prevalent unbelief of Spain and Italy and France, to a simulated faith, as when the priest turns atheist; or to open and defiant resistance[2]. The bitterness and narrowness of Christian controversialists, each anathematising the other, each insisting on his own definitions of the faith as essential conditions

---

[1] The *Nemesis of Faith*, published by Mr J. A. Froude in 1848, is now, I believe, out of print, and is probably not likely to be republished by its author. Taken together with the "Remains" of his brother R. H. Froude, it forms a comment almost as suggestive as the history of the two Newmans or the two Arnolds, on the history of religious thought in the last half century.

[2] Here again the general state of things in the countries where Rome exercises, or did exercise till lately, her most direct influence without the counter-check of an active and living Protestantism, finds a representative instance in the "Life of Blanco White."

of its having any power to save from sin or the penalties of sin, have deterred men from any thorough examination of the grounds of faith. They have not cared to undertake the preliminary enquiry where the path by which they travelled was to lead them, not into the fair field of truth, but into a labyrinth of thorns and briars[1]. You have known, I cannot doubt, as I have done, some who

---

[1] The state of feeling produced by the reciprocal denunciations of controversalists has found expression in Pope's familiar lines:

"For modes of faith let senseless bigots fight,
 His can't be wrong whose life is in the right."

It is suggestive that like lines in Dryden's *Religio Laici*,

"Faith is not built on disquisitions vain;
 The things we must believe are few and plain,"

were followed by his conversion to Rome, and the poem of *The Hind and the Panther*. Taylor's "Dedication" to his *Liberty of Prophesying* represents the same tendency to a Latitudinarianism like that which has become characteristic of modern thought. "Where then," he asks, after a survey of the Churches and sects of his time, "shall we fix our confidence or join communion? To pitch upon any one of these is to throw the dice, if salvation be to be had only in one of them, and that every error that by chance hath made a sect and is distinguished by a name is damnable." The whole treatise is given to working out the ideal of a Church which should impose no other term of communion than the Apostles' Creed. Baxter, in the closing years of his life, drew very near to a like wide comprehensiveness.

have thus made shipwreck of their faith, who, with great power and brilliant genius, have begun their career among you as the highest of high Churchmen, talking glibly of the notes of Catholicity, asserting the authority of the Church as against private judgment, quoting the Vincentian Canon of the "*Quod semper, quod ubique, quod ab omnibus*" as though it were applicable to the most disputable formulæ ; and you have seen after a year or two, it may be of great success in the regions of science or of culture, a strange and sad transformation. They appear as the destroyers of the faith which once they preached, and turn, almost as if with a personal vindictiveness, upon the Creed which had held them in bondage and trammelled the free exercise of their thought, as the enemy of civilisation and of science.

And then, secondly, there is yet another source of unbelief which I name, not that you may condemn others, but that you may judge yourselves. What St Paul noted as explaining the degradation of the race is true also—fatally true—of the degradation of the individual soul. Men do not care to retain God in their knowledge because they have ceased to honour Him as a Father and shrink from regarding Him as a judge[1]. They will not come to the light lest their deeds should be reproved. They hear the preacher reasoning of righteousness, temperance and judgment to come—and they, at first, put off the unwelcome task of acting on his words to the more convenient season which never comes—and then the wish is father to the thought—and they say in their hearts that there is no judgment and no God. Have you not felt that it is so? Have you not known, as you look back upon a year of selfishness and sensuality—upon some lavish act of sin which "lets in contagion to the inward parts," and leaves on the soul the indelible stain of a lost purity, that not your Reason, but your Will, rose up in rebellion against the Truth which you reject—that you looked round for arguments which might confirm you in your denial or your doubt—that having ceased to

[1] Rom. i. 19—29.

pray, you sought to convince yourselves that prayer was a delusive unreality. Conscience is not yet dead, and therefore you seek for the narcotic of speculative unbelief that it may drug you into at least a partial insensibility. If any of you have trodden that downward path you will do well to remember that it is not thus that the victories of Truth are won—that you enter on the enquiry with a mind set upon a foregone conclusion. The Masters of those who know—who, even if they are not for us, are yet not against us, will tell you that "self-reverence, self-knowledge, self-control" are the conditions of which your own poet speaks[1], as of "sovereign power" so of all clearness of spiritual perception. "Into a soul skilled in evil Wis-

---

[1] "Self-reverence, self-knowledge, self-control,
These three alone lead life to sovereign power,
Yet not for power—power of herself
Would come uncalled for, but to live by law,
Acting the law we live by without fear;
And because right is right, to follow right
Were wisdom in the scorn of consequence."
                    Tennyson's *Œnone*.

dom will not enter, nor dwell in the body that is subject unto sin [1]."

The attacks on the faith thus weakened, or the spiritual perception thus obscured, come from many different quarters, if not with the concert of an organised campaign, yet with a common aim. Criticism questions the date, or the authorship, or the accuracy of the Sacred Books; tells us that the records which purport to give the *Origines* of the faith of Israel or of Christendom are the product of a later age, marked, each of them, by human tendencies, or even party purposes, and that the *Origines* themselves are to be found in the cloudland of mythical tradition, with or without a nucleus of historical fact. Marks of compilation or editorship are found where before we had recognised only the work of a single hand. The diversities which present themselves in the presentation of our Lord's teaching in the Synoptic Gospels and St John's are urged as shewing that the last

---

[1] Wisd. of Sol. i. 4. The Greek word rendered in the English version as "malicious" is κακότεχνον.

is not the work of the beloved disciple, but of some unknown speculative thinker of the second century. Not a few of St Paul's Epistles are noted as being manifestly spurious, standing on the same footing as the Clementine Homilies. You, in this place, have materials ready at hand for giving in these matters a reason of the hope that is in you. You have been taught how the Bible took its place in the Church[1], after what siftings and searchings of evidence—after what test and trial of its spiritual power as the channel through which the Word of God was brought to the souls of men. You have seen how the parade of an enormous erudition, summing up what were alleged to be the results of an impartial criticism of the claims of a Supernatural Religion, has collapsed, like the shadowy phantom who poured into the ear of the sleeping mother of mankind

> distempered, discontented thoughts,
> Blown up with high conceits, engendering pride,

before the touch of an Ithuriel spear of more

---

[1] See Dr Westcott's *Bible in the Church*.

celestial temper[1]. You have been taught that in the midst of all the diversities of thought, temperament, tendencies, which mark the writings of the New Testament, there is a central unity—that no historical error has been proved against its records sufficient to invalidate their claim to our respect. And above all, you have learnt to examine these questions without panic and without passion, to admit the right of men to ask them, and not to judge them hastily if they seem to you to have answered the questions wrongly. You would not think that the foundations of the earth were out of course if the book of Ecclesiastes were shewn to be a dramatic personation of the character of the Son of David, like that which we recognise as such in the Wisdom of Solomon, or if the second Epistle of St Peter were proved to stand on a less firm basis of authority than the first.

Those who press the incompatibility of the results of scientific research with the re-

---

[1] See Dr Lightfoot's series of Papers on "Supernatural Religion" in the *Contemporary Review* for 1876-77.

cord of the creative work with which the book of Genesis opens, dwell in part on facts which are all but universally recognised, in part on theories which, whatever claim they may possess as approximate solutions of phenomena, stand, as yet, at best on the footing of ingenious, but unproved, hypotheses. No sane person would now quote texts against the conclusions which we identify with the names of Copernicus and Galileo and Newton. Few would venture to raise the cry of impiety against the geological theories that demand an almost limitless period for the preparation of the earth as the dwellingplace of man. We look with a pitying astonishment on the chronological tables which barely half a century ago fixed the creation of the world, sun, moon and stars, as well as earth, in the autumn of B.C. 4004[1]. The more recent theories of the evolution of all forms of life from some protoplasmic germs, of the origin of species, not by successive creative acts, but by the accumulation, through long ages, of variations singly

[1] Greswell's *Fasti Catholici*, I.

imperceptible, of the descent of man from some anthropoid ape, can scarcely claim as yet to be invested with the same authority. The history of the past has here, also, however, its lessons for the present. The zeal, "not according to knowledge," which condemned Galileo[1] and asserted in the early days of the British Association that the geological theories which we connect with the honoured name of Sedgwick were "incompatible with Christianity," and bore on them "the taint of infidelity[2]," may repeat the blunders of the former days, which in this respect were neither better nor worse than the latter. We need to examine these specu-

[1] Galileo's enforced recantation has been regarded by Roman Catholic theologians from very different standpoints. On the one hand some have found comfort in the thought that he was condemned by the Congregation of the Holy Office and not by the Pope personally, and that thus the Infallibility of the successor of St Peter was not compromised (Celeste's *Galileo*, c. XII.). On the other he has been praised as having made a sincere recantation (the "*E pur si muove*" being dismissed as a Protestant *mythos*), and so set a noble example of the submission of intellect to faith (Wetzer and Welter, *Kirchen-Lexikon*, Art. *Galilei*).

[2] Dean Cockburn, *The Bible defended against the British Association*, 1844.

lations also without prejudice and without passion, without the bitterness of condemnation, which has its source in panic while it simulates the confidence of faith. "Day unto day uttereth speech, night unto night declareth knowledge," and, should they also come to take their place, with missing links of evidence supplied, as demonstrable conclusions, we may welcome them as a true interpretation of the facts of God's universe, reconcilable, not, it may be, with the outward form and symbols of the truth which were adapted to an earlier stage in the history of mankind, but with the essential truth that underlies those symbols. Artificial schemes of reconciliation detail by detail, the *laissez faire* assumption that the works of God cannot contradict even the letter which we have identified with His word[1],—these we may

---

[1] The failure of such attempts, even in the hands of men like Buckland or Hugh Miller, is a warning against the hasty reproduction of these or like schemes in the future. It is doubtless a wiser course that the students of Theology and of Science should accept a partition treaty and work on in parallel lines independently of each other with mutual respect

leave to those who are wanting in the wider faith. Knowledge may grow from more to more, but the faith which rests on the eternal rock will keep pace with her advance. There was a creative energy manifested in every variation of type which worked out the Divine idea. When the anthropoid ape—if we were to admit the possibility of the transformation—first became a "being of large discourse looking before and after," a man endowed with reason, speech, conscience, will, there was that which answers to the record, veiled, it may be, in the symbols of the world's infancy, that God made man—Adam, the pro-

and sympathy. But to assume that the conclusions of science will ultimately be found to coincide with a natural and honest interpretation of the letter of Gen. i.—vi. rests on the further assumption, incapable of proof, that that record was intended to be an unerring scientific statement of the true history of the phenomena of the Universe; and a time may come, is indeed sure to come, when the students in the two regions will compare results and ask whether they agree. It is, I believe, a wiser and braver course to admit the possibility of disagreement, and to limit our thoughts of the Genesis records to the great central ideas which were in the mind of the human writer, ideas coming from the Eternal Spirit but clothing themselves in the symbols of a time of imperfect knowledge and the generalisations as of an infant Newton.

totype of humanity,—out of the dust of the ground, yet in His own image, and breathed into his nostrils the breath of life[1].

The attack advances from the outworks to the citadel, and Science—or those who prophesy in the name of Science—proclaim that there can be no revelation of the mind of God, because the idea of a revelation presupposes a miraculous interposition, and the order of Nature testifies against the possibility of miracles. That objection may be

---

[1] I find that I have almost reproduced unconsciously the very words in which the great Apostle of Evolution states the view which he, as might be expected, rejects. (Haeckel, *The Evolution of Man*, II. 458.) "These same dualistic philosophers must of course, if they are consistent, also assume that there will be a moment in the Phylogeny of the human mind at which this mind first entered the vertebrate body of man. Accordingly, at the time when the human body developed from the body of the Anthropoid Ape (thus probably in the latter part of the Tertiary Period) a specific human mind-element, or, as it is usually expressed, a "divine spark," must have suddenly entered, or been breathed into, the brain of the Anthropoid Ape and there have associated itself with the already existing Ape-mind. I need not point out the theoretic difficulties involved in this conception......Comparative Psychology, however, teaches that this frontier-post (Reason) between man and beast is altogether untenable."

urged, as you know, either on the ground of a scepticism pure and simple, contending that there can be no evidence adequate to prove a miracle against the overwhelming presumption from the uniformity of Nature, or from the higher ground of an ideal theism resting on the assumption that the maintenance of law, and not interference with it, is more worthy of our highest conceptions of the Divine Nature, and that, therefore, there is, from that standpoint also, a presumption against phenomena claiming to be miraculous[1]. Answers have been given to both those presumptions with a completeness which lies beyond my reach[2]. It has been urged as against the first

---

[1] Hume's *Essay on Miracles* may be taken as the representative of the one school, Goethe's assertion that the idea of a miracle was a blasphemy against the majesty of God, of the other.

[2] No thoughtful reader can study Dr Mozley's Bampton Lectures on Miracles without profound interest. But it may be questioned whether he too does not, like his predecessor Dean Mansel, tend to drift into a scepticism in the interests of orthodoxy when he maintains that a uniform succession of phenomena in the past gives no grounds for anticipating a like succession in the future. On the whole I fall back upon Butler's discussion of the Miraculous Element of

presumption, that there are phenomena in the natural world, exceptional and rare in their occurrence, which yet we receive, when they are attested by evidence that we should consider trustworthy in other cases, as coming within the range of law; that in order that the presumption might rest on an adequate basis, we need an induction from the history of other worlds like our own, and passing through similar stages of development. It has been contended, as against the second, that it introduces into our conception of God, the very anthropomorphism against which we have heard such indignant protests—that it juggles with ambiguous terms when it identifies the Law which conscience recognises as binding, with that which is but a convenient expression of the manner in which material phenomena succeed each other—that even from its own standpoint it would be true that, as man rises to his highest dignity when Will obeying Law, in its true sense, asserts its supremacy

Revelation (*Anal.* II. 2) as being less subtle but more satisfying.

over merely automatic actions, so there is no dishonour done to our ideal of God when we think of Him, also, as putting forth His Will, in accordance with the wisdom and with the love which, with Hooker, we may recognise as the true eternal Law of His being[1], even though in so doing He should break through what, in the other sense of the word, are the Laws which He has imposed on the world of Nature, which without that exercise of sovereignty, would be but an eternally automatic mechanism.

We are thus carried on one step further to the great question of all. Can we know that God is? Can we know what He is? Is He a rewarder of them that diligently seek Him? Does He govern the world in righteousness? Is He such that we should serve Him, love

---

[1] It may rightly be urged that on this view the Miracle itself (assuming adequate evidence of the fact) presupposes the law of uniform succession which it interrupts, and is itself the expression of the higher Law working now through that lower law, and now through its suspension. Of that higher Law itself it is true that it includes love, life, and will, and therefore that "her seat is the bosom of God, her voice the harmony of the world." (Hooker, *E. P. T. ad fin.*)

Him, yearn after His presence now, that to see and know Him as He is shall be hereafter the beatific vision of the Saints of God? Here also, as we know but too well, some of the keenest intellects and noblest natures of our time have made shipwreck of their faith. The words that "that which is knowable of God" is manifest in them, being intellectually apprehended from the things that are made, even His eternal power and Godhead, have come to seem to them as a voice heard in a dream and not audible to the waking ear. The laws of evidence or the constitution of men's minds have, it would seem, undergone a catastrophic change within the last hundred years. Paley's argument from design is out of date. "We cannot infer from the watch the existence of its maker. The very 'cunningest of Nature's clocks' may have been developed out of a ruder and rougher timepiece, and that, in its turn, may have originated in the spontaneous activity of some germ-cell more sensitive than its fellows, to the motion of the heavens which it measures. We, at all events, cannot even guess at the purpose and character of the maker. We must content ourselves with observing its movements, and taking its wheels and springs to pieces[1]. In that positive knowledge there is wisdom and safety. In the

---

[1] I have but summed up the very words of Huxley's *Lay Sermons*, p. 330. He is answering Paley's argument from the watch and the inferences of teleology generally, "Imagine that it had been possible to shew that all these changes had resulted first from a tendency in the structure to vary indefinitely, and secondly from something in the surrounding world which helped all variations in the direction of an accurate timekeeper and checked all those in other directions, then it is obvious that the force of Paley's argument would be gone, for it would be demonstrated that an apparatus thoroughly well adapted to a particular purpose might be the result of a method of trial and ends worked by unintelligent agents, as well as of the direct application of the means appropriate to that end by an intelligent agent." I confess, in spite of the undue depreciation which now rests on Paley's name (a natural reaction, it may be, from a period of undue honour), that I could wish for one hour of his robust common sense in answer to this "It is obvious," "it would be demonstrated." Does the inference that there is a Will that designs vary in the inverse ratio of the magnitude and complexity of the design? Assuming the theory of evolution to be carried backward and forward to the remotest periods of duration of which we can conceive, is it more philosophical to believe that it speaks of a Will that is, and was, and is to come, or to find in it no object of faith but a "tendency" and a "something"?

attempt to go beyond it we are going back to the childhood of the race, when it peopled earth and heaven with Unseen Powers, and bowed in blind terror or gratitude, before the presence of the supernatural. The *consensus* of mankind in the times of ignorance cannot be allowed to weigh against the illumination of the present." That conclusion of Atheism or Agnosticism has been contemplated with very different thoughts. There are those who see in it, like Lucretius[1], the last triumph of

[1] "Humana ante oculos foede cum vita jaceret
In terris oppressa gravi sub religione
Quae caput a caeli regionibus ostendebat,
Horribili super aspectu mortalibus instans,
Primum Graius homo mortalis tollere contra
Est oculos ausus primusque obsistere contra,
Quem nec fama deûm nec fulmina nec minitanti
Murmure compressit caelum, sed eo magis acrem
Inritat animi virtutem, effringere ut arta
Naturae primus portarum claustra cupiret.
Ergo vivida vis animi pervicit, et extra
Processit longe flammantia moenia mundi,
Atque omne immensum peragravit mente animoque.
Unde refert nobis victor quod possit oriri
Quid nequeat, finita potestas denique cuique
Quanam sit ratione atque alte terminus haerens,
Quare religio pedibus subjecta vicissim
Opteritur, nos exaequat victoria caelo."
  Lucret. *De Nat.* 1. 62—79.

the "*vivida vis animi*" which neither the "*fama deûm nec fulmina*" can terrify, over the Religion which has been the curse of the world's history. There are others whom it plunges, as in the vision of the German thinker[1], into the blackness of darkness. They "gaze on the immeasurable world for the Divine Eye, and it glares on them with an empty black bottomless eye-socket. They have laid them down to sleep, and they awaken in a stormy chaos, in the Everlasting Midnight, and there comes no morning, and no soft healing hand and no infinite Father." " Our little life is the sigh of Nature or only its echo. Mists fall and worlds reek up from

---

[1] Jean Paul Richter, *Siebenkäs*. I quote from Carlyle's *Miscellanies*, vol. II., p. 371—375 (ed. 1840). It adds to the almost terrific power of this vision of a world without God, that it is the Christ as the ideal representative of Humanity who is thus made to utter the blank despair of finding that His trust in the Father had been a delusive dream. Richter's own comment on what he had thus imagined is worth adding: "If ever my heart were to grow so wretched and so dead that all feelings in it which announce the being of a God were extinct there, I would terrify myself with this sketch of mine. It would heal me, and give me my feelings back" (p. 370).

the Sea of Death : the Future is a mounting mist, and the Present is a falling one." You and I, my friends, have to look on this picture and on that, and to ask the question, Have we indeed no Father? Is there indeed no God? If you deal honestly with your own spirits, if you do not close your eyes against the light, or narcotise the thoughts that accuse or else excuse each other, if you live by the light you have, even though it be but as the rays of a flickering torch shining through the mist and darkness, I have no fear for the result. I hold to the old belief that " The heavens declare the glory of God, and the firmament sheweth His handywork"— that the order of the universe testifies to a Divine purpose working through the ages to a result which shall testify, not of limited Power or imperfect Goodness, but of a Supreme Wisdom and Love victorious even over the freedom which seems to thwart them, that deep within the consciousness of each human soul there lies the capacity for knowing God, the promise and the potency of a higher and

Eternal Life. "He is not far from every one of us," and in the contrite heart and pure which He prefers above all temples, makes Himself manifest to those who diligently seek Him. Even from the scientific standpoint the phenomena of Theopathy[1] which thus

[1] I use the word as a comprehensive expression of the whole cycle of emotions which connect themselves with the belief that men are in contact and communion with the Eternal, that they have found God, and that He is the Father of their spirits. They are found, it will be acknowledged, in every age, in every race, under all conditions of knowledge and creed and culture. In Moses and David and Job and Paul and John, in Socrates and Plato, in Augustine and Bernard and Tauler and à Kempis, in Hooker and Leighton and Herbert and Keble and Maurice and Erskine, in Mahometan Mystics and English Quakers, in millions of men and women of whom the world was not worthy, but whom it has not known, they have been as the very central passion of their being. They have been found historically with greater purity and intensity within the range of the influences of Christendom, and in proportion as those influences have been allowed to act, than in those who saw the Light that lighteth every man through more refracting *media*. They have been united, in the vast majority of cases, with a greater purity and holiness than was found in their absence, with a manifest power alike to strengthen and to soothe. Humanity has appeared in its noblest ideal of excellence where they have most characterised it. What explanation has a merely materialistic science to offer of these phenomena? Are they all, from first to last, a delusion, a mockery and a snare? Are these also automatic functions of the grey matter of the brain, or abnormal developments of

present themselves, and which have been verified throughout the ages by experimental

hysteria? Or are they witnesses that this is indeed the goal and consummation to which man's nature tends and in which it finds its completeness?

It is obvious that it is on the reality of the grounds of these emotions that the whole question of the efficacy of prayer turns, and not on its power to produce changes in the outward phenomena of nature round us or in our material condition. We may ask for many things, and receive not, because we ask amiss. We may ask for health and prosperity, for rain and sunshine and plenteous harvests, and receive not, because it is better for us in the sum and total of things that we should be without that which we have asked for. We may ask and receive not, because we ask for that which comes under the dominion of a law which it is not the will of the Father to suspend or change, which, as soon as we know its existence, we recognise as wiser and better than any choice or wish of ours. But if we seek, not, as the Heathen seek, as Christians have too often sought, what we shall eat or what we shall drink or wherewithal we shall be clothed, but for the kingdom of God and His righteousness, there is surely a chorus of attestation that such prayers are answered. The crucial test of prayer would be found, not as suggested in the well-known letter to Dr Tyndall in the *Contemporary Review* (XX. p. 305), in a comparison of results as regards material success in one Hospital Ward, for the patients in which people were praying outside, with those in another Hospital for which people were not praying—(can we imagine, by the way, any one with a mind after the mind of Christ, praying that the sufferers in the latter might not recover, or leaving them, by an act of volition, unprayed for?) but in two Wards, in one of which the patients prayed for themselves and for each other as they have been taught by Christ to pray, while in the other, men had "nourished tests, crave for an explanation and a theory as much as those of the material universe or of our physical life. To those who go beyond that standpoint they will prepare the way for the fuller Apocalypse of all that may be known of God. To the worship of the Unknown and the Unknowable, leaving the

a blind life within the brain," and never known what it was to lift their hands in prayer. We need not fear the result of such an experiment. Phthisis and cancer might do their work in each, but in the one there would be, what physicians see too often, the picture of a lazar-house such as Milton has drawn :

> "Dire was the tossing, deep the groans: Despair
> Tended the sick, busiest from couch to couch;
> And over them triumphant Death his dart
> Shook, but delayed to strike, though oft invoked
> With vows as their chief good and final hope."
> *Par. Lost*, XI.

In the other there would be what also they, at least, sometimes see, patience, and joy, and hope, and the faith that all is well, and trust in the Father who scourgeth every son whom He receiveth, and the calm surrender of their own wills to His, and the readiness for death, or the willingness to remain. Are these lesser or greater goods than a rapid or slow recovery, than the healing of the burning fever or the fractured limb? Would not even the most dispassionate and sceptical practitioner admit that these presented, not by the violation of law, but by its natural working, at least more favourable conditions than the other for the action of his best chosen remedies, or the *vis medicatrix Naturæ ?*

world to itself, we oppose, in the full assurance of Faith, the worship of the Father and the Son and the Eternal Spirit—of God manifested in Christ and reconciling the world unto Himself.

THE END.

**Edited with Notes by Professor Plumptre.**

*The Mission of the Comforter.* By JULIUS CHARLES HARE, M.A., Archdeacon of Lewes. New Edition. Crown 8vo, 7s. 6d.

**Edited by Professor Plumptre.**

*The Victory of Faith.* By Archdeacon HARE. With Introductory Notices by Professor F. D. MAURICE and Dean STANLEY. New Edition. Crown 8vo, 6s. 6d.

---

WORKS BY THE
## REV. J. B. LIGHTFOOT, D.D.,
Bishop of Durham.

*St Paul's Epistles.* Revised Texts, with Introductions, Notes, &c.

    THE GALATIANS. Fifth Edition, 8vo, 12s.

    THE PHILIPPIANS. Fourth Edition, 8vo, 12s.

    THE COLOSSIANS and PHILEMON. Third Edition, 8vo, 12s.

*St Clement of Rome.* An Appendix, containing the newly recovered Portions. With Introductions, Notes, and Translation of the whole. 8vo, 8s. 6d.

*On a Fresh Revision of the English New Testament.* Second Edition. Crown 8vo, 6s.

---

MACMILLAN AND CO., LONDON.

## By CANON WESTCOTT, D.D.

*A General Survey of the History of the Canon of the New Testament during the First Four Centuries.* Third Edition, Revised. Crown 8vo, 10s. 6d.

*Introduction to the Study of the Gospels.* Fifth Edition. Crown 8vo, 10s. 6d.

*The Bible in the Church.* A Popular Account of the Collection and Reception of the Holy Scriptures in the Christian Churches. New Edition. 18mo, 4s. 6d.

*A General View of the History of the English Bible.* Second Edition. Crown 8vo, 10s. 6d.

*The Gospel of the Resurrection.* Thoughts on its Relations to Reason and History. New Edition. Crown 8vo, 6s.

*The Christian Life, manifold and one.* Six Sermons in Peterborough Cathedral. Crown 8vo, 2s. 6d.

*On the Religious Office of the Universities.* Sermons. Crown 8vo, 4s. 6d.

---

## By CANON FARRAR, D.D., F.R.S.

*Eternal Hope.* Sermons preached in Westminster Abbey, 1877. Crown 8vo, 6s.
[*Sixteenth Thousand.*

*Saintly Workers.* Lenten Lectures at St Andrew's, Holborn, 1878. Crown 8vo, 6s.

*In the Days of Thy Youth.* Sermons on Practical Subjects preached at Marlborough College, 1871-6. Third Edition. Crown 8vo, 9s.

*The Fall of Man: and other Sermons.* Third Edition. Crown 8vo, 6s.

*The Witness of History to Christ;* being the Hulsean Lectures for 1870. Fourth Edition. Crown 8vo, 5s.

*Seekers after God.* The Lives of Seneca, Epictetus, and Marcus Aurelius. New Edition. Crown 8vo, 6s.

*The Silence and Voices of God:* University and other Sermons. Third Edition. Crown 8vo, 6s.

---

MACMILLAN AND CO., LONDON.

*May*, 1879.

# A CATALOGUE of THEOLOGICAL BOOKS, with a Short Account of their Character and Aim,

Published by

## MACMILLAN AND CO.

*Bedford Street, Strand, London, W.C.*

---

**Abbott (Rev. E. A.)**—Works by the Rev. E. A. ABBOTT, D.D., Head Master of the City of London School:

BIBLE LESSONS. Second Edition. Crown 8vo. 4s. 6d.

"*Wise, suggestive, and really profound initiation into religious thought.*" —Guardian. *The Bishop of St. David's, in his speech at the Education Conference at Abergwilly, says he thinks* "*nobody could read them without being the better for them himself, and being also able to see how this difficult duty of imparting a sound religious education may be effected.*"

THE GOOD VOICES: A Child's Guide to the Bible. With upwards of 50 Illustrations. Crown 8vo. cloth gilt. 5s.

"*It would not be easy to combine simplicity with fulness and depth of meaning more successfully than Mr. Abbott has done.*"—Spectator. *The Times says*—"*Mr. Abbott writes with clearness, simplicity, and the deepest religious feeling.*"

CAMBRIDGE SERMONS PREACHED BEFORE THE UNIVERSITY. Second Edition. 8vo. 6s.

10,000 : 5 : 79.

**ABBOTT (Rev. E. A.)**—*continued.*

THROUGH NATURE TO CHRIST; or, The Ascent of Worship through Illusion to the Truth. 8vo. 12*s.* 6*d.*

"*The beauty of its style, its tender feeling, and its perfect sympathy, the originality and suggestiveness of many of its thoughts, would of themselves go far to recommend it. But far besides these, it has a certain value in its bold, comprehensive, trenchant method of apology, and in the adroitness with which it turns the flank of the many modern fallacies that caricature in order to condemn Christianity.*"—Church Quarterly Review.

**Ainger (Rev. Alfred).**—SERMONS PREACHED IN THE TEMPLE CHURCH. By the Rev. ALFRED AINGER, M.A. of Trinity Hall, Cambridge, Reader at the Temple Church. Extra fcap. 8vo. 6*s.*

"*It is,*" *the* British Quarterly *says*, "*the fresh unconventional talk of a clear independent thinker, addressed to a congregation of thinkers. . . . Thoughtful men will be greatly charmed by this little volume.*"

**Alexander.**—THE LEADING IDEAS of the GOSPELS. Five Sermons preached before the University of Oxford in 1870—71. By WILLIAM ALEXANDER, D.D., Brasenose College; Lord Bishop of Derry and Raphoe; Select Preacher. Cr. 8vo. 4*s.* 6*d.*

"*Eloquence and force of language, clearness of statement, and a hearty appreciation of the grandeur and importance of the topics upon which he writes, characterize his sermons.*"—Record.

**Arnold.**—Works by MATTHEW ARNOLD:

A BIBLE READING FOR SCHOOLS. THE GREAT PROPHECY OF ISRAEL'S RESTORATION (Isaiah, Chapters 40—66). Arranged and Edited for Young Learners. By MATTHEW ARNOLD, D.C.L., formerly Professor of Poetry in the University of Oxford, and Fellow of Oriel. Third Edition. 18mo. cloth. 1*s.*

*The* Times *says*—"*Whatever may be the fate of this little book in Government Schools, there can be no doubt that it will be found excellently calculated to further instruction in Biblical literature in any school into which it may be introduced. . . . We can safely say that whatever school uses this book, it will enable its pupils to understand Isaiah, a great advantage compared with other establishments which do not avail themselves of it.*"

ISAIAH XL.—LXVI., with the Shorter Prophecies allied to it. Arranged and Edited with Notes. Crown 8vo. 5*s.*

**Bather.**—ON SOME MINISTERIAL DUTIES, CATECHISING, PREACHING, &c. Charges by the late Archdeacon BATHER. Edited, with Preface, by Dr. C. J. VAUGHAN. Extra fcap. 8vo. 4*s.* 6*d.*

**Benham.**—A COMPANION TO THE LECTIONARY, being a Commentary on the Proper Lessons for Sundays and Holydays. By the Rev. W. BENHAM, B.D., Vicar of Margate. Cheaper Edition. Crown 8vo. 6s.

"*A very useful book. Mr. Benham has produced a good and welcome companion to our revised Lectionary. Its contents will, if not very original or profound, prove to be sensible and practical, and often suggestive to the preacher and the Sunday School teacher. They will also furnish some excellent Sunday reading for private hours.*"—Guardian.

**Bernard.**—THE PROGRESS OF DOCTRINE IN THE NEW TESTAMENT. By THOMAS D. BERNARD, M.A., Rector of Walcot and Canon of Wells. Third and Cheaper Edition. Crown 8vo. 5s. (Bampton Lectures for 1864.)

"*We lay down these lectures with a sense not only of being edified by sound teaching and careful thought, but also of being gratified by conciseness and clearness of expression and elegance of style.*"—Churchman.

**Binney.**—SERMONS PREACHED IN THE KING'S WEIGH HOUSE CHAPEL, 1829—69. By THOMAS BINNEY, D.D. New and Cheaper Edition. Extra fcap. 8vo. 4s. 6d.

"*Full of robust intelligence, of reverent but independent thinking on the most profound and holy themes, and of earnest practical purpose.*"—London Quarterly Review.

A SECOND SERIES OF SERMONS. Edited, with Biographical and Critical Sketch, by the Rev. HENRY ALLON, D.D. With Portrait of Dr. Binney engraved by JEENS. 8vo. 12s.

**Birks.**—Works by T. R. BIRKS, M.A., Professor of Moral Philosophy, Cambridge:

THE DIFFICULTIES OF BELIEF in connection with the Creation and the Fall, Redemption and Judgment. Second Edition, enlarged. Crown 8vo. 5s.

AN ESSAY ON THE RIGHT ESTIMATION OF MSS. EVIDENCE IN THE TEXT OF THE NEW TESTAMENT. Crown 8vo. 3s. 6d.

COMMENTARY ON THE BOOK OF ISAIAH, Critical, Historical and Prophetical; including a Revised English Translation. With Introduction and Appendices on the Nature of Scripture Prophecy, the Life and Times of Isaiah, the Genuineness of the Later Prophecies, the Structure and History of the whole Book, the Assyrian History in Isaiah's Days, and various Difficult Passages. Second Edition, revised. 8vo. 12s. 6d.

SUPERNATURAL REVELATION, or First Principles of Moral Theology. 8vo. 8s.

**Bradby.**—SERMONS PREACHED AT HAILEYBURY.
By E. H. BRADBY, M.A., Master. 8vo. 10s. 6d.

"*He who claims a public hearing now, speaks to an audience accustomed to Cotton, Temple, Vaughan, Bradley, Butler, Farrar, and others...... Each has given us good work, several, work of rare beauty, force, or originality; but we doubt whether any one of them has touched deeper chords, or brought more freshness and strength into his sermons, than the last of their number, the present Head Master of Haileybury.*"—Spectator.

**Butcher.**—THE ECCLESIASTICAL CALENDAR; its Theory and Construction. By SAMUEL BUTCHER, D.D., late Bishop of Meath. 4to. 14s.

**Butler (G.)**—Works by the Rev. GEORGE BUTLER, M.A., Principal of Liverpool College:

FAMILY PRAYERS. Crown 8vo. 5s.

*The prayers in this volume are all based on passages of Scripture—the morning prayers on Select Psalms, those for the evening on portions of the New Testament.*

SERMONS PREACHED in CHELTENHAM COLLEGE CHAPEL. Crown 8vo. 7s. 6d.

**Butler (Rev. H. M.)**—SERMONS PREACHED in the CHAPEL OF HARROW SCHOOL. By H. MONTAGU BUTLER, Head Master. Crown 8vo. 7s. 6d.

"*These sermons are adapted for every household. There is nothing more striking than the excellent good sense with which they are imbued.*"—Spectator.

A SECOND SERIES. Crown 8vo. 7s. 6d.

"*Excellent specimens of what sermons should be—plain, direct, practical, pervaded by the true spirit of the Gospel, and holding up lofty aims before the minds of the young.*"—Athenæum.

**Butler (Rev. W. Archer).**—Works by the Rev. WILLIAM ARCHER BUTLER, M.A., late Professor of Moral Philosophy in the University of Dublin:

SERMONS, DOCTRINAL AND PRACTICAL. Edited, with a Memoir of the Author's Life, by THOMAS WOODWARD, Dean of Down. With Portrait. Ninth Edition. 8vo. 8s.

*The Introductory Memoir narrates in considerable detail and with much interest, the events of Butler's brief life; and contains a few specimens of his poetry, and a few extracts from his addresses and essays, including a long and eloquent passage on the Province and Duty of the Preacher.*

## THEOLOGICAL BOOKS. 5

**BUTLER** (Rev. W. Archer)—*continued*.
A SECOND SERIES OF SERMONS. Edited by J. A. JEREMIE, D.D., Dean of Lincoln. Seventh Edition. 8vo. 7s.

*The* North British Review *says, " Few sermons in our language exhibit the same rare combination of excellencies; imagery almost as rich as Taylor's; oratory as vigorous often as South's; judgment as sound as Barrow's; a style as attractive but more copious, original, and forcible than Atterbury's; piety as elevated as Howe's, and a fervour as intense at times as Baxter's. Mr. Butler's are the sermons of a true poet."*

LETTERS ON ROMANISM, in reply to Dr. Newman's Essay on Development. Edited by the Dean of Down. Second Edition, revised by Archdeacon HARDWICK. 8vo. 10s. 6d.

*These Letters contain an exhaustive criticism of Dr. Newman's famous " Essay on the Development of Christian Doctrine." " A work which ought to be in the Library of every student of Divinity."*—BP. ST. DAVID'S.

**Campbell.**—Works by JOHN M'LEOD CAMPBELL:
THE NATURE OF THE ATONEMENT AND ITS RELATION TO REMISSION OF SINS AND ETERNAL LIFE. Fourth and Cheaper Edition, crown 8vo. 6s.

*"Among the first theological treatises of this generation."*—Guardian.
*" One of the most remarkable theological books ever written."*—Times.

CHRIST THE BREAD OF LIFE. An Attempt to give a profitable direction to the present occupation of Thought with Romanism. Second Edition, greatly enlarged. Crown 8vo. 4s. 6d.

*" Deserves the most attentive study by all who interest themselves in the predominant religious controversy of the day."*—Spectator.

REMINISCENCES AND REFLECTIONS, referring to his Early Ministry in the Parish of Row, 1825—31. Edited with an Introductory Narrative by his Son, DONALD CAMPBELL, M.A., Chaplain of King's College, London. Crown 8vo. 7s. 6d.

*These 'Reminiscences and Reflections,' written during the last year of his life, were mainly intended to place on record thoughts which might prove helpful to others. " We recommend this book cordially to all who are interested in the great cause of religious reformation."*—Times.
*" There is a thoroughness and depth, as well as a practical earnestness, in his grasp of each truth on which he dilates, which make his reflections very valuable."*—Literary Churchman.

THOUGHTS ON REVELATION, with Special Reference to the Present Time. Second Edition. Crown 8vo. 5s.

**CAMPBELL (J. M'Leod)**—*continued.*

RESPONSIBILITY FOR THE GIFT OF ETERNAL LIFE. Compiled by permission of the late J. M'LEOD CAMPBELL, D.D., from Sermons preached chiefly at Row in 1829—31. Crown 8vo. 5s.

"*There is a healthy tone as well as a deep pathos not often seen in sermons. His words are weighty and the ideas they express tend to perfection of life.*"—Westminster Review.

**Campbell (Lewis).**—SOME ASPECTS OF THE CHRISTIAN IDEAL. Sermons by the Rev. L. CAMPBELL, M.A., LL.D., Professor of Greek in the University of Glasgow. Crown 8vo. 6s.

**Canterbury.**—Works by ARCHIBALD CAMPBELL, Archbishop of Canterbury:

THE PRESENT POSITION OF THE CHURCH OF ENGLAND. Seven Addresses delivered to the Clergy and Churchwardens of his Diocese, as his Charge, at his Primary Visitation, 1872. Third Edition. 8vo. cloth. 3s. 6d.

SOME THOUGHTS ON THE DUTIES OF THE ESTABLISHED CHURCH OF ENGLAND AS A NATIONAL CHURCH. Seven Addresses delivered at his Second Visitation. 8vo. 4s. 6d.

**Cheyne.**—Works by T. K. CHEYNE, M.A., Fellow of Balliol College, Oxford:

THE BOOK OF ISAIAH CHRONOLOGICALLY ARRANGED. An Amended Version, with Historical and Critical Introductions and Explanatory Notes. Crown 8vo. 7s. 6d.

*The* Westminster Review *speaks of it as "a piece of scholarly work, very carefully and considerately done." The* Academy *calls it "a successful attempt to extend a right understanding of this important Old Testament writing."*

NOTES AND CRITICISMS on the HEBREW TEXT OF ISAIAH. Crown 8vo. 2s. 6d.

**Choice Notes on the Four Gospels,** drawn from Old and New Sources. Crown 8vo. 4s. 6d. each Vol. (St. Matthew and St. Mark in one Vol. price 9s.)

**Church.**—Works by the Very Rev. R. W. CHURCH, M.A., D.C.L., Dean of St. Paul's:

ON SOME INFLUENCES OF CHRISTIANITY UPON NATIONAL CHARACTER. Three Lectures delivered in St. Paul's Cathedral, Feb. 1873. Crown 8vo. 4s. 6d.

## THEOLOGICAL BOOKS. 7

**CHURCH (Very Rev. R. W.)**—*continued.*
"*Few books that we have met with have given us keener pleasure than this....... It would be a real pleasure to quote extensively, so wise and so true, so tender and so discriminating are Dean Church's judgments, but the limits of our space are inexorable. We hope the book will be bought.*"
—Literary Churchman.

THE SACRED POETRY OF EARLY RELIGIONS. Two Lectures in St. Paul's Cathedral. 18mo. 1s. I. The Vedas. II. The Psalms.

ST. ANSELM. Second Edition. Crown 8vo. 6s.
"*It is a sketch by the hand of a master, with every line marked by taste, learning, and real apprehension of the subject.*"—Pall Mall Gazette.

HUMAN LIFE AND ITS CONDITIONS. Sermons preached before the University of Oxford, 1876—78, with Three Ordination Sermons. Crown 8vo. 6s.

**Clergyman's Self-Examination concerning the** APOSTLES' CREED. Extra fcap. 8vo. 1s. 6d.

**Colenso.**—THE COMMUNION SERVICE FROM THE BOOK OF COMMON PRAYER; with Select Readings from the Writings of the Rev. F. D. MAURICE, M.A. Edited by the Right Rev. J. W. COLENSO, D.D., Lord Bishop of Natal. New Edition. 16mo. 2s. 6d.

**Collects of the Church of England.** With a beautifully Coloured Floral Design to each Collect, and Illuminated Cover. Crown 8vo. 12s. Also kept in various styles of morocco.
*The distinctive characteristic of this edition is the coloured floral design which accompanies each Collect, and which is generally emblematical of the character of the day or saint to which it is assigned; the flowers which have been selected are such as are likely to be in bloom on the day to which the Collect belongs.* The Guardian *thinks it "a successful attempt to associate in a natural and unforced manner the flowers of our fields and gardens with the course of the Christian year.*"

**Congreve.**—HIGH HOPES, AND PLEADINGS FOR A REASONABLE FAITH, NOBLER THOUGHTS, LARGER CHARITY. Sermons preached in the Parish Church of Tooting Graveney, Surrey. By J. CONGREVE, M.A., Rector. Cheaper Issue. Crown 8vo. 5s.

**Cotton.**—Works by the late GEORGE EDWARD LYNCH COTTON, D.D., Bishop of Calcutta:

**COTTON** (Bishop)—*continued.*

SERMONS PREACHED TO ENGLISH CONGREGATIONS IN INDIA. Crown 8vo. 7s. 6d.

EXPOSITORY SERMONS ON THE EPISTLES FOR THE SUNDAYS OF THE CHRISTIAN YEAR. Two Vols. Crown 8vo. 15s.

**Curteis.**—DISSENT in its RELATION to the CHURCH OF ENGLAND. Eight Lectures preached before the University of Oxford, in the year 1871, on the foundation of the late Rev. John Bampton, M.A., Canon of Salisbury. By GEORGE HERBERT CURTEIS, M.A., late Fellow and Sub-Rector of Exeter College; Principal of the Lichfield Theological College, and Prebendary of Lichfield Cathedral; Rector of Turweston, Bucks. New Edition. Crown 8vo. 7s. 6d.

"*Mr. Curteis has done good service by maintaining in an eloquent, temperate, and practical manner, that discussion among Christians is really an evil, and that an intelligent basis can be found for at least a proximate union.*"—Saturday Review. "*A well timed, learned, and thoughtful book.*"

**Davies.**—Works by the Rev. J. LLEWELYN DAVIES, M.A., Rector of Christ Church, St. Marylebone, etc.:

THE GOSPEL AND MODERN LIFE; with a Preface on a Recent Phase of Deism. Second Edition. To which is added Morality according to the Sacrament of the Lord's Supper, or Three Discourses on the Names, Eucharist, Sacrifice, and Communion. Extra fcap. 8vo. 6s.

WARNINGS AGAINST SUPERSTITION, IN FOUR SERMONS FOR THE DAY. Extra fcap. 8vo. 2s. 6d.

"*We have seldom read a wiser little book. The Sermons are short, terse, and full of true spiritual wisdom, expressed with a lucidity and a moderation that must give them weight even with those who agree least with their author....... Of the volume as a whole it is hardly possible to speak with too cordial an appreciation.*"—Spectator.

THE CHRISTIAN CALLING. Sermons. Extra fcap. 8vo. 6s.

**Donaldson.**—THE APOSTOLICAL FATHERS: a Critical Account of their Genuine Writings and of their Doctrines. By JAMES DONALDSON, LL.D. Crown 8vo. 7s. 6d.

**DONALDSON (J., LL.D.)**—*continued.*

*This book was published in 1864 as the first volume of a 'Critical History of Christian Literature and Doctrine from the death of the Apostles to the Nicene Council.' The intention was to carry down the history continuously to the time of Eusebius, and this intention has not been abandoned. But as the writers can be sometimes grouped more easily according to subject or locality than according to time, it is deemed advisable to publish the history of each group separately. The Introduction to the present volume serves as an introduction to the whole period.*

**Drake.**—THE TEACHING OF THE CHURCH DURING THE FIRST THREE CENTURIES ON THE DOCTRINES OF THE CHRISTIAN PRIESTHOOD AND SACRIFICE. By the Rev. C. B. DRAKE, M.A., Warden of the Church of England Hall, Manchester. Crown 8vo. 4s. 6d.

**Eadie.**—Works by JOHN EADIE, D.D., LL.D., Professor of Biblical Literature and Exegesis, United Presbyterian Church:

THE ENGLISH BIBLE. An External and Critical History of the various English Translations of Scripture, with Remarks on the Need of Revising the English New Testament. Two vols. 8vo. 28s.

"*Accurate, scholarly, full of completest sympathy with the translators and their work, and marvellously interesting.*"—Literary Churchman.

"*The work is a very valuable one. It is the result of vast labour, sound scholarship, and large erudition.*"—British Quarterly Review.

ST. PAUL'S EPISTLES TO THE THESSALONIANS. A Commentary on the Greek Text. Edited by the Rev. W. YOUNG, M.A., with a Preface by the Rev. Professor CAIRNS, D.D. 8vo. 12s.

**Ecce Homo.** A SURVEY OF THE LIFE AND WORK OF JESUS CHRIST. Fourteenth Edition. Crown 8vo. 6s.

"*A very original and remarkable book, full of striking thought and delicate perception; a book which has realised with wonderful vigour and freshness the historical magnitude of Christ's work, and which here and there gives us readings of the finest kind of the probable motive of His individual words and actions.*"—Spectator. "*The best and most established believer will find it adding some fresh buttresses to his faith.*"—Literary Churchman. "*If we have not misunderstood him, we have before us a writer who has a right to claim deference from those who think deepest and know most.*"—Guardian.

**Faber.**—SERMONS AT A NEW SCHOOL. By the Rev. ARTHUR FABER, M.A., Head Master of Malvern College. Cr. 8vo. 6s.

"*These are high-toned, earnest Sermons, orthodox and scholarlike, and laden with encouragement and warning, wisely adapted to the needs of school-life.*"—Literary Churchman.

**Farrar.**—Works by the Rev. F. W. FARRAR, D.D., F.R.S., Canon of Westminster, late Head Master of Marlborough College:

THE FALL OF MAN, AND OTHER SERMONS. Third Edition. Crown 8vo. 6s.

*The* Nonconformist *says of these Sermons, "Mr. Farrar's Sermons are almost perfect specimens of one type of Sermons, which we may concisely call beautiful. The style of expression is beautiful—there is beauty in the thoughts, the illustrations, the allusions—they are expressive of genuinely beautiful perceptions and feelings." The* British Quarterly *says, "Ability, eloquence, scholarship, and practical usefulness, are in these Sermons combined in a very unusual degree."*

THE WITNESS OF HISTORY TO CHRIST. Being the Hulsean Lectures for 1870. Fourth Edition. Crown 8vo. 5s.

*The following are the subjects of the Five Lectures:—I. "The Antecedent Credibility of the Miraculous." II. "The Adequacy of the Gospel Records." III. "The Victories of Christianity." IV. "Christianity and the Individual." V. "Christianity and the Race." The subjects of the four Appendices are:—A. "The Diversity of Christian Evidences." B. "Confucius." C. "Buddha." D. "Comte."*

SEEKERS AFTER GOD. The Lives of Seneca, Epictetus, and Marcus Aurelius. New Edition. Crown 8vo. 6s.

"*A very interesting and valuable book.*"—Saturday Review.

THE SILENCE AND VOICES OF GOD: University and other Sermons. Third Edition. Crown 8vo. 6s.

"*We can most cordially recommend Dr. Farrar's singularly beautiful volume of Sermons...... For beauty of diction, felicity of style, aptness of illustration and earnest loving exhortation, the volume is without its parallel.*"—John Bull. "*They are marked by great ability, by an honesty which does not hesitate to acknowledge difficulties and by an earnestness which commands respect.*"—Pall Mall Gazette.

"IN THE DAYS OF THY YOUTH." Sermons on Practical Subjects, preached at Marlborough College from 1871—76. Third Edition. Crown 8vo. 9s.

**FARRAR (Rev. F. W.)**—*continued.*

*"All Dr. Farrar's peculiar charm of style is apparent here, all that care and subtleness of analysis, and an even-added distinctness and clearness of moral teaching, which is what every kind of sermon wants, and especially a sermon to boys."*—Literary Churchman.

    ETERNAL HOPE. Five Sermons preached in Westminster Abbey, in 1876. With Preface, Notes, etc. Contents: What Heaven is.—Is Life Worth Living?—'Hell,' What it is not.—Are there few that be saved?—Earthly and Future Consequences of Sin. Sixteenth Thousand. Crown 8vo. 6s.

    SAINTLY WORKERS. Lenten Lectures delivered in St. Andrew's, Holborn, March and April, 1878. Crown 8vo. 6s.

**Fellowship:** LETTERS ADDRESSED TO MY SISTER MOURNERS. Fcap. 8vo. cloth gilt. 3s. 6d.

**Ferrar.**—A COLLECTION OF FOUR IMPORTANT MSS. OF THE GOSPELS, viz., 13, 69, 124, 346, with a view to prove their common origin, and to restore the Text of their Archetype. By the late W. H. FERRAR, M.A., Professor of Latin in the University of Dublin. Edited by T. K. ABBOTT, M.A., Professor of Biblical Greek, Dublin. 4to., half morocco. 10s. 6d.

**Forbes.**—Works by GRANVILLE H. FORBES, Rector of Broughton:
    THE VOICE OF GOD IN THE PSALMS. Cr. 8vo. 6s. 6d.

    VILLAGE SERMONS. By a Northamptonshire Rector. Crown 8vo. 6s.

*"Such a volume as the present . . . is as great an accession to the cause of a deep theology as the most refined exposition of its fundamental principles . . . We heartily accept his actual teaching as a true picture of what revelation teaches us, and thank him for it as one of the most profound that was ever made perfectly simple and popular . . . . It is part of the beauty of these sermons that while they apply the old truth to the new modes of feeling they seem to preserve the whiteness of its simplicity . . . . There will be plenty of critics to accuse this volume of inadequacy of doctrine because it says no more than Scripture about vicarious suffering and external retribution. For ourselves we welcome it most cordially as expressing adequately what we believe to be the true burden of the Gospel in a manner which may take hold either of the least or the most cultivated intellect."*—Spectator.

**Hardwick.**—Works by the Ven. ARCHDEACON HARDWICK: CHRIST AND OTHER MASTERS. A Historical Inquiry into some of the Chief Parallelisms and Contrasts between Christianity and the Religious Systems of the Ancient World. New Edition, revised, and a Prefatory Memoir by the Rev. FRANCIS PROCTER, M.A. New Edition. Cr. 8vo. 10s. 6d.

*The plan of the work is boldly and almost nobly conceived. . . . We commend it to the perusal of all those who take interest in the study of ancient mythology, without losing their reverence for the supreme authority of the oracles of the living God."*—Christian Observer.

A HISTORY OF THE CHRISTIAN CHURCH. Middle Age. From Gregory the Great to the Excommunication of Luther, Edited by WILLIAM STUBBS, M.A., Regius Professor of Modern History in the University of Oxford. With Four Maps constructed for this work by A. KEITH JOHNSTON. New Edition. Crown 8vo. 10s. 6d.

*"As a Manual for the student of ecclesiastical history in the Middle Ages, we know no English work which can be compared to Mr. Hardwick's book."*—Guardian.

A HISTORY of the CHRISTIAN CHURCH DURING THE REFORMATION. New Edition, revised by Professor STUBBS. Crown 8vo. 10s. 6d.

*This volume is intended as a sequel and companion to the "History of the Christian Church during the Middle Age."*

**Hare.**—Works by the late ARCHDEACON HARE:

THE VICTORY OF FAITH. By JULIUS CHARLES HARE, M.A., Archdeacon of Lewes. Edited by Prof. PLUMPTRE. With Introductory Notices by the late Prof. MAURICE and Dean STANLEY. Third Edition. Crown 8vo. 6s. 6d.

THE MISSION OF THE COMFORTER. With Notes. New Edition, edited by Prof. E. H. PLUMPTRE. Crn. 8vo. 7s. 6d.

**Harris.**—SERMONS. By the late GEORGE COLLYER HARRIS, Prebendary of Exeter, and Vicar of St. Luke's, Torquay. With Memoir by CHARLOTTE M. YONGE, and Portrait. Extra fcap. 8vo. 6s.

**Hervey.**—THE GENEALOGIES OF OUR LORD AND SAVIOUR JESUS CHRIST, as contained in the Gospels of St. Matthew and St. Luke, reconciled with each other, and shown to be in harmony with the true Chronology of the Times. By Lord ARTHUR HERVEY, Bishop of Bath and Wells. 8vo. 10s. 6d.

**Hort.**—TWO DISSERTATIONS. I. On ΜΟΝΟΓΕΝΗΣ ΘΕΟΣ in Scripture and Tradition. II. On the "Constantinopolitan" Creed and other Eastern Creeds of the Fourth Century. By F. J. A. HORT, D.D., Fellow and Divinity Lecturer of Emmanuel College, Cambridge. 8vo. 7s. 6d.

**Howson (Dean)**—Works by:
BEFORE THE TABLE. An Inquiry, Historical and Theological, into the True Meaning of the Consecration Rubric in the Communion Service of the Church of England. By the Very Rev. J. S. HOWSON, D.D., Dean of Chester. With an Appendix and Supplement containing Papers by the Right Rev. the Bishop of St. Andrew's and the Rev. R. W. KENNION, M.A. 8vo. 7s. 6d.

THE POSITION OF THE PRIEST DURING CONSECRATION IN THE ENGLISH COMMUNION SERVICE. A Supplement and a Reply. Crown 8vo. 2s. 6d.

**Hymni Ecclesiæ.**—Fcap. 8vo. 7s. 6d.
*This collection was edited by Dr. Newman while he lived at Oxford.*

**Hyacinthe.**—CATHOLIC REFORM. By FATHER HYACINTHE. Letters, Fragments, Discourses. Translated by Madame HYACINTHE-LOYSON. With a Preface by the Very Rev. A. P. STANLEY, D.D., Dean of Westminster. Cr. 8vo. 7s. 6d.
"*A valuable contribution to the religious literature of the day, and is especially opportune at a time when a controversy of no ordinary importance upon the very subject it deals with is engaged in all over Europe.*"—Daily Telegraph.

**Imitation of Christ.**—FOUR BOOKS. Translated from the Latin, with Preface by the Rev. W. BENHAM, B.D., Vicar of Margate. Printed with Borders in the Ancient Style after Holbein, Dürer, and other Old Masters. Containing Dances of Death, Acts of Mercy, Emblems, and a variety of curious ornamentation. Cr. 8vo. gilt edges. 7s. 6d.

**Jacob.**—BUILDING IN SCIENCE, AND OTHER SERMONS. By J. A. JACOB, M.A., Minister of St. Thomas's, Paddington. Extra fcap. 8vo. 6s.

**Jellett.**—THE EFFICACY OF PRAYER: being the Donnellan Lectures for 1877. By J. H. JELLETT, B.D., Senior Fellow of Trinity College, Dublin, formerly President of the Royal Irish Academy. Second Edition. 8vo. 5s.

**Jennings and Lowe.**—THE PSALMS, with Introductions and Critical Notes. By A. C. JENNINGS, B.A., Jesus College, Cambridge, Tyrwhitt Scholar, Crosse Scholar, Hebrew University Scholar, and Fry Scholar of St. John's College; helped in parts by W. H. LOWE, M.A., Hebrew Lecturer and late Scholar of Christ's College, Cambridge, and Tyrwhitt Scholar. Complete in two vols. crown 8vo. 10s. 6d. each. Vol. 1, Psalms i.—lxxii., with Prolegomena; Vol. 2, Psalms lxxiii.—cl.

**Killen.**—THE ECCLESIASTICAL HISTORY OF IRELAND from the Earliest Period to the Present Time. By W. D. KILLEN, D.D., President of Assembly's College, Belfast, and Professor of Ecclesiastical History. Two vols. 8vo. 25s.

"*Those who have the leisure will do well to read these two volumes. They are full of interest, and are the result of great research.*"—Spectator.

**Kingsley.**—Works by the late Rev. CHARLES KINGSLEY, M.A., Rector of Eversley, and Canon of Westminster:

THE WATER OF LIFE, AND OTHER SERMONS. New Edition. Crown 8vo. 6s.

THE GOSPEL OF THE PENTATEUCH; AND DAVID. New Edition. Crown 8vo. 6s.

GOOD NEWS OF GOD. Eighth Edition. Crown 8vo. 6s.

SERMONS FOR THE TIMES. New Edition. Crown 8vo. 6s.

VILLAGE AND TOWN AND COUNTRY SERMONS. New Edition. Crown 8vo. 6s.

SERMONS on NATIONAL SUBJECTS. Second Edition. Fcap. 8vo. 3s. 6d.

THE KING OF THE EARTH, and other Sermons, a Second Series of Sermons on National Subjects. Second Edition. Fcap. 8vo. 3s. 6d.

DISCIPLINE, AND OTHER SERMONS. Second Edition. Fcap. 8vo. 3s. 6d.

WESTMINSTER SERMONS. With Preface. New Edition. Crown 8vo. 6s.

**Kynaston.**—SERMONS PREACHED IN THE COLLEGE CHAPEL, CHELTENHAM, during the First Year of his Office. By the Rev. HERBERT KYNASTON, M.A., Principal of Cheltenham College. Crown 8vo. 6s.

**Lightfoot.**—Works by J. B. LIGHTFOOT, D.D., Bishop of Durham.

S. PAUL'S EPISTLE TO THE GALATIANS. A Revised Text, with Introduction, Notes, and Dissertations. Fifth Edition, revised. 8vo. cloth. 12s.

While the Author's object has been to make this commentary generally complete, he has paid special attention to everything relating to St. Paul's personal history and his intercourse with the Apostles and Church of the Circumcision, as it is this feature in the Epistle to the Galatians which has given it an overwhelming interest in recent theological controversy. The Spectator says, " There is no commentator at once of sounder judgment and more liberal than Dr. Lightfoot."

ST. PAUL'S EPISTLE TO THE PHILIPPIANS. A Revised Text, with Introduction, Notes, and Dissertations. Fourth Edition, revised. 8vo. 12s.

"No commentary in the English language can be compared with it in regard to fulness of information, exact scholarship, and laboured attempts to settle everything about the epistle on a solid foundation."—Athenæum.

ST. PAUL'S EPISTLES TO THE COLOSSIANS AND TO PHILEMON. A Revised Text with Introduction, Notes, etc. Third Edition, revised. 8vo. 12s.

" It bears marks of continued and extended reading and research, and of ampler materials at command. Indeed, it leaves nothing to be desired by those who seek to study thoroughly the epistles contained in it, and to do so with all known advantages presented in sufficient detail and in convenient form."—Guardian.

S. CLEMENT OF ROME. An Appendix containing the newly discovered portions of the two Epistles to the Corinthians with Introductions and Notes, and a Translation of the whole. 8vo. 8s. 6d.

ON A FRESH REVISION OF THE ENGLISH NEW TESTAMENT. Second Edition. Crown 8vo. 6s.

The Author shews in detail the necessity for a fresh revision of the authorized version on the following grounds:—1. False Readings. 2. Artificial distinctions created. 3. Real distinctions obliterated. 4. Faults of Grammar. 5. *Faults of Lexicography.* 6. *Treatment of Proper Names, official titles, etc.* 7. *Archaisms, defects in the English, errors of the press, etc.* "*The book is marked by careful scholarship, familiarity with the subject, sobriety, and circumspection.*"—Athenæum.

**Lorne.**—THE PSALMS LITERALLY RENDERED IN VERSE. By the MARQUIS OF LORNE. With three Illustrations. New Edition. Crown 8vo. 7s. 6d.

**Luckock.**—THE TABLES OF STONE. A Course of Sermons preached in All Saints' Church, Cambridge, by H. M. LUCKOCK, M.A., Canon of Ely. Fcap. 8vo. 3s. 6d.

**Maclaren.**—SERMONS PREACHED at MANCHESTER. By ALEXANDER MACLAREN. Sixth Edition. Fcap. 8vo. 4s. 6d.

*These Sermons represent no special school, but deal with the broad principles of Christian truth, especially in their bearing on practical, every day life. A few of the titles are:*—"*The Stone of Stumbling,*" "*Love and Forgiveness,*" "*The Living Dead,*" "*Memory in Another World,*" "*Faith in Christ,*" "*Love and Fear,*" "*The Choice of Wisdom,*" "*The Food of the World.*"

A SECOND SERIES OF SERMONS. Fourth Edition. Fcap. 8vo. 4s. 6d.

*The* Spectator *characterises them as "vigorous in style, full of thought, rich in illustration, and in an unusual degree interesting."*

A THIRD SERIES OF SERMONS. Third Edition. Fcap. 8vo. 4s. 6d.

"*Sermons more sober and yet more forcible, and with a certain wise and practical spirituality about them it would not be easy to find.*"—Spectator.

WEEK-DAY EVENING ADDRESSES. Delivered in Manchester. Extra Fcap. 8vo. 2s. 6d.

**Maclear.**—Works by the Rev. G. F. MACLEAR, D.D., Head Master of King's College School :

A CLASS-BOOK OF OLD TESTAMENT HISTORY. With Four Maps. New Edition. 18mo. 4s. 6d.

"*The present volume,*" *says the Preface,* "*forms a Class-Book of Old Testament History from the Earliest Times to those of Ezra and Nehemiah. In its preparation the most recent authorities have been consulted, and wherever it has appeared useful, Notes have been subjoined illustrative of the Text, and, for the sake of more advanced students, references*

**MACLEAR (Dr. G. F.)**—*continued.*
*added to larger works. The Index has been so arranged as to form a concise Dictionary of the Persons and Places mentioned in the course of the Narrative." The Maps, prepared by Stanford, materially add to the value and usefulness of the book.* The British Quarterly Review *calls it "A careful and elaborate, though brief compendium of all that modern research has done for the illustration of the Old Testament. We know of no work which contains so much important information in so small a compass."*

### A CLASS-BOOK OF NEW TESTAMENT HISTORY.
Including the Connexion of the Old and New Testament. New Edition. 18mo. 5s. 6d.

*The present volume forms a sequel to the Author's Class-Book of Old Testament History, and continues the narrative to the close of S. Paul's second imprisonment at Rome. The work is divided into three Books— I. The Connection between the Old and New Testament. II. The Gospel History. III. The Apostolic History. In the Appendix are given Chronological Tables.* The Clerical Journal *says, "It is not often that such an amount of useful and interesting matter on biblical subjects, is found in so convenient and small a compass, as in this well-arranged volume."*

### A CLASS-BOOK OF THE CATECHISM OF THE CHURCH OF ENGLAND. New and Cheaper Edition. 18mo. 1s. 6d.

*The present work is intended as a sequel to the two preceding books. "Like them, it is furnished with notes and references to larger works, and it is hoped that it may be found, especially in the higher forms of our Public Schools, to supply a suitable manual of instruction in the chief doctrines of our Church, and a useful help in the preparation of Candidates for Confirmation."* The Literary Churchman *says, "It is indeed the work of a scholar and divine, and as such, though extremely simple, it is also extremely instructive. There are few clergy who would not find it useful in preparing Candidates for Confirmation; and there are not a few who would find it useful to themselves as well."*

### A FIRST CLASS-BOOK OF THE CATECHISM OF THE CHURCH OF ENGLAND, with Scripture Proofs for Junior Classes and Schools. New Edition. 18mo. 6d.

*This is an epitome of the larger Class-book, meant for junior students and elementary classes. The book has been carefully condensed, so as to contain clearly and fully, the most important part of the contents of the larger book.*

**MACLEAR** (Dr. G. F.)—*continued.*

**A SHILLING-BOOK of OLD TESTAMENT HISTORY.**
New Edition. 18mo. cloth limp. 1s.

*This Manual bears the same relation to the larger Old Testament History, that the book just mentioned does to the larger work on the Catechism. It consists of Ten Books, divided into short chapters, and subdivided into sections, each section treating of a single episode in the history, the title of which is given in bold type.*

**A SHILLING-BOOK of NEW TESTAMENT HISTORY.**
New Edition. 18mo. cloth limp. 1s.

**A MANUAL OF INSTRUCTION FOR CONFIRMATION AND FIRST COMMUNION,** with Prayers and Devotions. 32mo. cloth extra, red edges. 2s.

*This is an enlarged and improved edition of 'The Order of Confirmation.' To it have been added the Communion Office, with Notes and Explanations, together with a brief form of Self Examination and Devotions selected from the works of Cosin, Ken, Wilson, and others.*

**THE ORDER OF CONFIRMATION,** with Prayers and Devotions. 32mo. cloth. 6d.

**THE FIRST COMMUNION,** with Prayers and Devotions for the Newly Confirmed. 32mo. 6d.

**THE HOUR OF SORROW;** or, The Order for the Burial of the Dead. With Prayers and Hymns. 32mo. cloth extra. 2s.

**APOSTLES OF MEDIÆVAL EUROPE.** Cr. 8vo. 4s. 6d.

*In two Introductory Chapters the author notices some of the chief characteristics of the mediæval period itself; gives a graphic sketch of the devastated state of Europe at the beginning of that period, and an interesting account of the religions of the three great groups of vigorous barbarians—the Celts, the Teutons, and the Sclaves—who had, wave after wave, overflowed its surface. He then proceeds to sketch the lives and work of the chief of the courageous men who devoted themselves to the stupendous task of their conversion and civilization, during a period extending from the 5th to the 13th century; such as St. Patrick, St. Columba, St. Columbanus, St. Augustine of Canterbury, St. Boniface, St. Olaf, St. Cyril, Raymond Sull, and others. "Mr. Maclear will have done a great work if his admirable little volume shall help to break up the dense ignorance which is still prevailing among people at large."*—Literary Churchman.

**Macmillan.**—Works by the Rev. HUGH MACMILLAN, LL.D., F.R.S.E. (For other Works by the same Author, see CATALOGUE OF TRAVELS and SCIENTIFIC CATALOGUE).

**MACMILLAN (Rev. H., LL.D.)**—*continued.*

THE TRUE VINE; or, the Analogies of our Lord's Allegory. Third Edition. Globe 8vo. 6s.

*The* Nonconformist *says, "It abounds in exquisite bits of description, and in striking facts clearly stated." The* British Quarterly *says, "Readers and preachers who are unscientific will find many of his illustrations as valuable as they are beautiful."*

BIBLE TEACHINGS IN NATURE. Twelfth Edition. Globe 8vo. 6s.

*In this volume the author has endeavoured to shew that the teaching of Nature and the teaching of the Bible are directed to the same great end; that the Bible contains the spiritual truths which are necessary to make us wise unto salvation, and the objects and scenes of Nature are the pictures by which these truths are illustrated. "He has made the world more beautiful to us, and unsealed our ears to voices of praise and messages of love that might otherwise have been unheard."*—British Quarterly Review. *"Dr. Macmillan has produced a book which may be fitly described as one of the happiest efforts for enlisting physical science in the direct service of religion."*—Guardian.

THE SABBATH OF THE FIELDS. A Sequel to "Bible Teachings in Nature." Second Edition. Globe 8vo. 6s.

*"This volume, like all Dr. Macmillan's productions, is very delightful reading, and of a special kind. Imagination, natural science, and religious instruction are blended together in a very charming way."*—British Quarterly Review.

THE MINISTRY OF NATURE. Fourth Edition. Globe 8vo. 6s.

*"Whether the reader agree or not with his conclusions, he will acknowledge he is in the presence of an original and thoughtful writer."*—Pall Mall Gazette. *"There is no class of educated men and women that will not profit by these essays."*—Standard.

OUR LORD'S THREE RAISINGS FROM THE DEAD. Globe 8vo. 6s.

**M'Clellan.**—THE NEW TESTAMENT. A New Translation on the Basis of the Authorised Version, from a Critically revised Greek Text, with Analyses, copious References and Illustrations from original authorities, New Chronological and Analytical Harmony of the Four Gospels, Notes and Dissertations. A contribution to Christian Evidence. By JOHN BROWN M'CLELLAN, M.A., late Fellow of Trinity College, Cambridge. In Two

**M'CLELLAN (J. B.)**—*continued.*

Vols. Vol. I.—The Four Gospels with the Chronological and Analytical Harmony. 8vo. 30*s.*

"*One of the most remarkable productions of recent times,*" says the Theological Review, "*in this department of sacred literature;*" and the British Quarterly Review *terms it* "*a thesaurus of first-hand investigations.*" "*Of singular excellence, and sure to make its mark on the criticism of the New Testament.*"—John Bull.

**Maurice.**—Works by the late Rev. F. DENISON MAURICE, M.A., Professor of Moral Philosophy in the University of Cambridge:

*The* Spectator *says,—"Few of those of our own generation whose names will live in English history or literature have exerted so profound and so permanent an influence as Mr. Maurice."*

THE PATRIARCHS AND LAWGIVERS OF THE OLD TESTAMENT. Third and Cheaper Edition. Crown 8vo. 5*s.*

*The Nineteen Discourses contained in this volume were preached in the chapel of Lincoln's Inn during the year* 1851. *The texts are taken from the books of Genesis, Exodus, Numbers, Deuteronomy, Joshua, Judges, and Samuel, and involve some of the most interesting biblical topics discussed in recent times.*

THE PROPHETS AND KINGS OF THE OLD TESTAMENT. Third Edition, with new Preface. Crown 8vo. 10*s.* 6*d.*

*Mr. Maurice, in the spirit which animated the compilers of the Church Lessons, has in these Sermons regarded the Prophets more as preachers of righteousness than as mere predictors—an aspect of their lives which, he thinks, has been greatly overlooked in our day, and than which, there is none we have more need to contemplate. He has found that the Old Testament Prophets, taken in their simple natural sense, clear up many of the difficulties which beset us in the daily work of life; make the past intelligible, the present endurable, and the future real and hopeful.*

THE GOSPEL OF THE KINGDOM OF HEAVEN. A Series of Lectures on the Gospel of St. Luke. Crown 8vo. 9*s.*

*Mr. Maurice, in his Preface to these Twenty-eight Lectures, says,—"In these Lectures I have endeavoured to ascertain what is told us respecting the life of Jesus by one of those Evangelists who proclaim Him to be the Christ, who says that He did come from a Father, that He did baptize with the Holy Spirit, that He did rise from the dead. I have chosen the*

MAURICE (Rev. F. D.)—*continued.*

one who is most directly connected with the later history of the Church, who was not an Apostle, who professedly wrote for the use of a man already instructed in the faith of the Apostles. I have followed the course of the writer's narrative, not changing it under any pretext. I have adhered to his phraseology, striving to avoid the substitution of any other for his."

### THE GOSPEL OF ST. JOHN. A Series of Discourses.
Third and Cheaper Edition. Crown 8vo. 6s.

*The* Literary Churchman *thus speaks of this volume:* "*Thorough honesty, reverence, and deep thought pervade the work, which is every way solid and philosophical, as well as theological, and abounding with suggestions which the patient student may draw out more at length for himself.*"

### THE EPISTLES OF ST. JOHN. A Series of Lectures
on Christian Ethics. Second and Cheaper Edition. Cr. 8vo. 6s.

*These Lectures on Christian Ethics were delivered to the students of the Working Men's College, Great Ormond Street, London, on a series of Sunday mornings. Mr. Maurice believes that the question in which we are most interested, the question which most affects our studies and our daily lives, is the question, whether there is a foundation for human morality, or whether it is dependent upon the opinions and fashions of different ages and countries. This important question will be found amply and fairly discussed in this volume, which the* National Review *calls "Mr. Maurice's most effective and instructive work. He is peculiarly fitted by the constitution of his mind, to throw light on St. John's writings." Appended is a note on "Positivism and its Teacher."*

### EXPOSITORY SERMONS ON THE PRAYER-BOOK.
The Prayer-book considered especially in reference to the Romish System. Second Edition. Fcap. 8vo. 5s. 6d.

*After an Introductory Sermon, Mr. Maurice goes over the various parts of the Church Service, expounds in eighteen Sermons, their intention and significance, and shews how appropriate they are as expressions of the deepest longings and wants of all classes of men.*

### WHAT IS REVELATION? A Series of Sermons on the
Epiphany; to which are added, Letters to a Theological Student on the Bampton Lectures of Mr. Mansel. Crown 8vo. 10s. 6d.

*Both Sermons and Letters were called forth by the doctrine maintained by Mr. Mansel in his Bampton Lectures, that Revelation cannot be a direct Manifestation of the Infinite Nature of God. Mr. Maurice maintains*

**MAURICE (Rev. F. D.)**—*continued.*

the opposite doctrine, and in his Sermons explains why, in spite of the high authorities on the other side, he must still assert the principle which he discovers in the Services of the Church and throughout the Bible.

**SEQUEL TO THE INQUIRY, "WHAT IS REVELATION?"** Letters in Reply to Mr. Mansel's Examination of "Strictures on the Bampton Lectures." Crown 8vo. 6s.

*This, as the title indicates, was called forth by Mr. Mansel's examination of Mr. Maurice's Strictures on his doctrine of the Infinite.*

**THEOLOGICAL ESSAYS.** Third Edition. Crown 8vo. 10s. 6d.

"The book," says Mr. Maurice, "expresses thoughts which have been working in my mind for years; the method of it has not been adopted carelessly; even the composition has undergone frequent revision." There are seventeen Essays in all, and although meant primarily for Unitarians, to quote the words of the Clerical Journal, "it leaves untouched scarcely any topic which is in agitation in the religious world; scarcely a moot point between our various sects; scarcely a plot of debateable ground between Christians and Infidels, between Romanists and Protestants, between Socinians and other Christians, between English Churchmen and Dissenters on both sides. Scarce is there a misgiving, a difficulty, an aspiration stirring amongst us now—now, when men seem in earnest as hardly ever before about religion, and ask and demand satisfaction with a fearlessness which seems almost awful when one thinks what is at stake—which is not recognised and grappled with by Mr. Maurice."

**THE DOCTRINE OF SACRIFICE DEDUCED FROM THE SCRIPTURES.** Crown 8vo. 7s. 6d.

**THE RELIGIONS OF THE WORLD, AND THEIR RELATIONS TO CHRISTIANITY.** Fifth Edition. Crown 8vo. 5s.

**ON THE LORD'S PRAYER.** Fourth Edition. Fcap. 8vo. 2s. 6d.

**ON THE SABBATH DAY**; the Character of the Warrior, and on the Interpretation of History. Fcap. 8vo. 2s. 6d.

**THE LORD'S PRAYER, THE CREED, AND THE COMMANDMENTS.** A Manual for Parents and Schoolmasters. To which is added the Order of the Scriptures. 18mo. cloth limp. 1s.

**DIALOGUES ON FAMILY WORSHIP.** Crown 8vo. 6s.

**MAURICE** (Rev. F. D.)—*continued.*

**SOCIAL MORALITY.** Twenty-one Lectures delivered in the University of Cambridge. New and Cheaper Edition. Cr. 8vo. 10s. 6d.

"*Whilst reading it we are charmed by the freedom from exclusiveness and prejudice, the large charity, the loftiness of thought, the eagerness to recognise and appreciate whatever there is of real worth extant in the world, which animates it from one end to the other. We gain new thoughts and new ways of viewing things, even more, perhaps, from being brought for a time under the influence of so noble and spiritual a mind.*"
—Athenæum.

**THE CONSCIENCE:** Lectures on Casuistry, delivered in the University of Cambridge. Second and Cheaper Edition. Crown 8vo. 5s.

*The* Saturday Review *says: "We rise from the perusal of these lectures with a detestation of all that is selfish and mean, and with a living impression that there is such a thing as goodness after all."*

**LECTURES ON THE ECCLESIASTICAL HISTORY OF THE FIRST AND SECOND CENTURIES.** 8vo. 10s. 6d.

**LEARNING AND WORKING.** Six Lectures delivered in Willis's Rooms, London, in June and July, 1854.—THE RELIGION OF ROME, and its Influence on Modern Civilisation. Four Lectures delivered in the Philosophical Institution of Edinburgh, in December, 1854. Crown 8vo. 5s.

**SERMONS PREACHED IN COUNTRY CHURCHES.** Crown 8vo. 10s. 6d.

"*Earnest, practical, and extremely simple.*"—Literary Churchman. "*Good specimens of his simple and earnest eloquence. The Gospel incidents are realized with a vividness which we can well believe made the common people hear him gladly. Moreover they are sermons which must have done the hearers good.*"—John Bull.

**Moorhouse.**—Works by JAMES MOORHOUSE, M.A., Bishop of Melbourne:

**SOME MODERN DIFFICULTIES RESPECTING** the FACTS OF NATURE AND REVELATION. Fcap. 8vo. 2s. 6d.

**JACOB.** Three Sermons preached before the University of Cambridge in Lent 1870. Extra fcap. 8vo. 3s. 6d.

**O'Brien.**—PRAYER. Five Sermons preached in the Chapel of Trinity College, Dublin. By JAMES THOMAS O'BRIEN, D.D., Bishop of Ossory and Ferns. 8vo. 6s.

"*It is with much pleasure and satisfaction that we render our humble tribute to the value of a publication whose author deserves to be remembered with such deep respect.*"—Church Quarterly Review.

**Palgrave.**—HYMNS. By FRANCIS TURNER PALGRAVE. Third Edition, enlarged. 18mo. 1s. 6d.

*This is a collection of twenty original Hymns*, which the Literary Churchman *speaks of as " so choice, so perfect, and so refined,—so tender in feeling, and so scholarly in expression."*

**Paul of Tarsus.** An Inquiry into the Times and the Gospel of the Apostle of the Gentiles. By a GRADUATE. 8vo. 10s. 6d.

"*Turn where we will throughout the volume, we find the best fruit of patient inquiry, sound scholarship, logical argument, and fairness of conclusion. No thoughtful reader will rise from its perusal without a real and lasting profit to himself, and a sense of permanent addition to the cause of truth.*"—Standard.

**Philochristus.**—MEMOIRS OF A DISCIPLE OF THE LORD. Second Edition. 8vo. 12s.

"*The winning beauty of this book and the fascinating power with which the subject of it appeals to all English minds will secure for it many readers.*"—Contemporary Review.

**Picton.**—THE MYSTERY OF MATTER; and other Essays. By J. ALLANSON PICTON, Author of "New Theories and the Old Faith." Cheaper Edition. With New Preface. Crown 8vo. 6s.

*Contents*— The Mystery of Matter: The Philosophy of Ignorance: The Antithesis of Faith and Sight: The Essential Nature of. Religion: Christian Pantheism.

**Plumptre.**—MOVEMENTS IN RELIGIOUS THOUGHT. Sermons preached before the University of Cambridge, Lent Term, 1879. By E. H. PLUMPTRE, D.D., Professor of Divinity, King's College, London, Prebendary of St. Paul's, etc. Fcap. 8vo. 3s. 6d.

**Prescott.**—THE THREEFOLD CORD. Sermons preached before the University of Cambridge. By J. E. PRESCOTT, B.D. Fcap. 8vo. 3s. 6d.

**Procter.**—A HISTORY OF THE BOOK OF COMMON PRAYER: With a Rationale of its Offices. By FRANCIS PROCTER, M.A. Thirteenth Edition, revised and enlarged. Cr. 8vo. 10s. 6d.

The Athenæum *says:*—"*The origin of every part of the Prayer-book has been diligently investigated,—and there are few questions or facts connected with it which are not either sufficiently explained, or so referred to that persons interested may work out the truth for themselves.*"

**Procter and Maclear.**—AN ELEMENTARY INTRODUCTION TO THE BOOK OF COMMON PRAYER. Re-arranged and Supplemented by an Explanation of the Morning and Evening Prayer and the Litany. By F. PROCTER, M.A., and G. F. MACLEAR, D.D. New Edition. Enlarged by the addition of the Communion Service and the Baptismal and Confirmation Offices. 18mo. 2s. 6d.

*The Literary Churchman characterizes it as " by far the completest and most satisfactory book of its kind we know. We wish it were in the hands of every schoolboy and every schoolmaster in the kingdom."*

**Psalms of David** CHRONOLOGICALLY ARRANGED. An Amended Version, with Historical Introductions and Explanatory Notes. By FOUR FRIENDS. Second and Cheaper Edition, much enlarged. Crown 8vo. 8s. 6d.

*One of the chief designs of the Editors, in preparing this volume, was to restore the Psalter as far as possible to the order in which the Psalms were written. They give the division of each Psalm into strophes, and of each strophe into the lines which composed it, and amend the errors of translation. The* Spectator *calls it "one of the most instructive and valuable books that have been published for many years."*

**Psalter (Golden Treasury).**—THE STUDENT'S EDITION. Being an Edition of the above with briefer Notes. 18mo. 3s. 6d.

*The aim of this edition is simply to put the reader as far as possible in possession of the plain meaning of the writer. "It is a gem," the* Nonconformist *says.*

**Pulsford.**—SERMONS PREACHED IN TRINITY CHURCH, GLASGOW. By WILLIAM PULSFORD, D.D. Cheaper Edition. Crown 8vo. 4s. 6d.

**Ramsay.**—THE CATECHISER'S MANUAL; or, the Church Catechism Illustrated and Explained, for the Use of Clergymen, Schoolmasters, and Teachers. By ARTHUR RAMSAY, M.A. Second Edition. 18mo. 1s. 6d.

**Rays of Sunlight for Dark Days.** A Book of Selections for the Suffering. With a Preface by C. J. VAUGHAN, D.D. 18mo. Eighth Edition. 3s. 6d. Also in morocco, old style.

*Dr. Vaughan says in the Preface, after speaking of the general run of Books of Comfort for Mourners, "It is because I think that the little volume now offered to the Christian sufferer is one of greater wisdom and of deeper experience, that I have readily consented to the request that I would introduce it by a few words of Preface." The book consists of a series of very brief extracts from a great variety of authors, in prose and poetry, suited to the many moods of a mourning or suffering mind. "Mostly gems of the first water."*—Clerical Journal.

**Reynolds.**—NOTES OF THE CHRISTIAN LIFE. A Selection of Sermons by HENRY ROBERT REYNOLDS, B.A., President of Cheshunt College, and Fellow of University College, London. Crown 8vo. 7s. 6d.

**Roberts.**—DISCUSSIONS ON THE GOSPELS. By the Rev. ALEXANDER ROBERTS, D.D. Second Edition, revised and enlarged. 8vo. 16s.

**Robinson.**—MAN IN THE IMAGE OF GOD; and other Sermons preached in the Chapel of the Magdalen, Streatham, 1874—76. By H. G. ROBINSON, M.A., Prebendary of York. Crown 8vo. 7s. 6d.

**Romanes.**—CHRISTIAN PRAYER AND GENERAL LAWS, being the Burney Prize Essay for 1873. With an Appendix, examining the views of Messrs. Knight, Robertson, Brooke, Tyndall, and Galton. By GEORGE J. ROMANES, M.A. Crown 8vo. 5s.

**Salmon.**—THE REIGN OF LAW, and other Sermons, preached in the Chapel of Trinity College, Dublin. By the Rev. GEORGE SALMON, D.D., Regius Professor of Divinity in the University of Dublin. Crown 8vo. 6s.

*"Well considered, learned, and powerful discourses."*—Spectator.

**Sanday.**—THE GOSPELS IN THE SECOND CENTURY. An Examination of the Critical part of a Work entitled "Supernatural Religion." By WILLIAM SANDAY, M.A., late Fellow of Trinity College, Oxford. Crown 8vo. 8s. 6d.

*"A very important book for the critical side of the question as to the authenticity of the New Testament, and it is hardly possible to conceive a writer of greater fairness, candour, and scrupulousness."*—Spectator.

**Selborne.**—THE BOOK OF PRAISE: From the Best English Hymn Writers. Selected and arranged by Lord SELBORNE. With Vignette by WOOLNER. 18mo. 4s. 6d.

**SELBORNE (Lord)**—*continued.*

*It has been the Editor's desire and aim to adhere strictly, in all cases in which it could be ascertained, to the genuine uncorrupted text of the authors themselves. The names of the authors and date of composition of the hymns, when known, are affixed, while notes are added to the volume, giving further details. The Hymns are arranged according to subjects.*
"*There is not room for two opinions as to the value of the 'Book of Praise.'*"
—Guardian. "*Approaches as nearly as one can conceive to perfection.*"
—Nonconformist.

BOOK OF PRAISE HYMNAL. *See* end of this Catalogue.

**Service.**—SALVATION HERE AND HEREAFTER. Sermons and Essays. By the Rev. JOHN SERVICE, D.D., Minister of Inch. Fourth Edition. Crown 8vo. 6s.

"*We have enjoyed to-day a rare pleasure, having just closed a volume of sermons which rings true metal from title page to finis, and proves that another and very powerful recruit has been added to that small band of ministers of the Gospel who are not only abreast of the religious thought of their time, but have faith enough and courage enough to handle the questions which are the most critical, and stir men's minds most deeply, with frankness and thoroughness.*"—Spectator.

**Shipley.**—A THEORY ABOUT SIN, in relation to some Facts of Daily Life. Lent Lectures on the Seven Deadly Sins. By the Rev. ORBY SHIPLEY, M.A. Crown 8vo. 7s. 6d.

"*Two things Mr. Shipley has done, and each of them is of considerable worth. He has grouped these sins afresh on a philosophic principle..... and he has applied the touchstone to the facts of our moral life... so wisely and so searchingly as to constitute his treatise a powerful antidote to self-deception.*"—Literary Churchman.

**Smith.**—PROPHECY A PREPARATION FOR CHRIST. Eight Lectures preached before the University of Oxford, being the Bampton Lectures for 1869. By R. PAYNE SMITH, D.D., Dean of Canterbury. Second and Cheaper Edition. Crown 8vo. 6s.

*The author's object in these Lectures is to shew that there exists in the Old Testament an element, which no criticism on naturalistic principles can either account for or explain away: that element is Prophecy. The author endeavours to prove that its force does not consist merely in its predictions.* "*These Lectures overflow with solid learning.*"—Record.

**Smith.**—CHRISTIAN FAITH. Sermons preached before the University of Cambridge. By W. SAUMAREZ SMITH, M.A., Principal of St. Aidan's College, Birkenhead. Fcap. 8vo. 3s. 6d.

**Stanley.**—Works by the Very Rev. A. P. STANLEY, D.D., Dean of Westminster:

THE ATHANASIAN CREED, with a Preface on the General Recommendations of the RITUAL COMMISSION. Cr. 8vo. 2s.

"*Dr. Stanley puts with admirable force the objections which may be made to the Creed; equally admirable, we think, in his statement of its advantages.*"—Spectator.

THE NATIONAL THANKSGIVING. Sermons preached in Westminster Abbey. Second Edition. Crown 8vo. 2s. 6d.

ADDRESSES AND SERMONS AT ST. ANDREW'S in 1872, 1875 and 1876. Crown 8vo. 5s.

**Stewart and Tait.**—THE UNSEEN UNIVERSE; or, Physical Speculations on a Future State. By Professors BALFOUR STEWART and P. G. TAIT. Sixth Edition, Revised and Enlarged. Crown 8vo. 6s.

"*A most remarkable and most interesting volume, which, probably more than any that has appeared in modern times, will affect religious thought on many momentous questions—insensibly it may be, but very largely and very beneficially.*"—Church Quarterly. "*This book is one which well deserves the attention of thoughtful and religious readers...... It is a perfectly safe enquiry, on scientific grounds, into the possibilities of a future existence.*"—Guardian.

**Swainson.**—Works by C. A. SWAINSON, D.D., Canon of Chichester:

THE CREEDS OF THE CHURCH in their Relations to Holy Scripture and the Conscience of the Christian 8vo. cloth. 9s.

THE AUTHORITY OF THE NEW TESTAMENT, and other LECTURES, delivered before the University of Cambridge. 8vo. cloth. 12s.

**Taylor.**—THE RESTORATION OF BELIEF. New and Revised Edition. By ISAAC TAYLOR, Esq. Crown 8vo. 8s. 6d.

**Temple.**—SERMONS PREACHED IN THE CHAPEL of RUGBY SCHOOL. By F. TEMPLE, D.D., Bishop of Exeter. New and Cheaper Edition. Extra fcap. 8vo. 4s. 6d.

*This volume contains Thirty-five Sermons on topics more or less intimately connected with every-day life. The following are a few of the subjects discoursed upon:*—"*Love and Duty;*" "*Coming to Christ;*"

TEMPLE (Dr.)—*continued*.

"*Great Men;*" "*Faith;*" "*Doubts;*" "*Scruples;*" "*Original Sin;*" "*Friendship;*" "*Helping Others;*" "*The Discipline of Temptation;*" "*Strength a Duty;*" "*Worldliness;*" "*Ill Temper;*" "*The Burial of the Past.*"

A SECOND SERIES OF SERMONS PREACHED IN THE CHAPEL OF RUGBY SCHOOL. Second Edition. Extra fcap. 8vo. 6s.

*This Second Series of Forty-two brief, pointed, practical Sermons, on topics intimately connected with the every-day life of young and old, will be acceptable to all who are acquainted with the First Series. The following are a few of the subjects treated of:—"Disobedience," "Almsgiving," "The Unknown Guidance of God," "Apathy one of our Trials," "High Aims in Leaders," "Doing our Best," "The Use of Knowledge," "Use of Observances," "Martha and Mary," "John the Baptist," "Severity before Mercy," "Even Mistakes Punished," "Morality and Religion," "Children," "Action the Test of Spiritual Life," "Self-Respect," "Too Late," "The Tercentenary."*

A THIRD SERIES OF SERMONS PREACHED IN RUGBY SCHOOL CHAPEL IN 1867—1869. Extra fcap. 8vo. 6s.

*This Third Series of Bishop Temple's Rugby Sermons, contains thirty-six brief discourses, including the "Good-bye" sermon preached on his leaving Rugby to enter on the office he now holds.*

Thring.—Works by Rev. EDWARD THRING, M.A.:

SERMONS DELIVERED AT UPPINGHAM SCHOOL. Crown 8vo. 5s.

THOUGHTS ON LIFE-SCIENCE. New Edition, enlarged and revised. Crown 8vo. 7s. 6d.

Trench.—Works by R. CHENEVIX TRENCH, D.D., Archbishop of Dublin:

NOTES ON THE PARABLES OF OUR LORD. Thirteenth Edition. 8vo. 12s.

*This work has taken its place as a standard exposition and interpretation of Christ's Parables. The book is prefaced by an Introductory Essay in four chapters:—I. On the definition of the Parable. II. On Teaching by Parables. III. On the Interpretation of the Parables. IV. On other Parables besides those in the Scriptures. The author then proceeds to take up the Parables one by one, and by the aid of philology, history, antiquities, and the researches of travellers, shews forth the significance,*

**TRENCH (Archbishop)**—*continued.*

*beauty, and applicability of each, concluding with what he deems its true moral interpretation. In the numerous Notes are many valuable references, illustrative quotations, critical and philological annotations, etc., and appended to the volume is a classified list of fifty-six works on the Parables.*

### NOTES ON THE MIRACLES OF OUR LORD. Eleventh Edition, revised. 8vo. 12s.

*In the 'Preliminary Essay' to this work, all the momentous and interesting questions that have been raised in connection with Miracles, are discussed with considerable fulness. The Essay consists of six chapters:—I. On the Names of Miracles,* i.e. *the Greek words by which they are designated in the New Testament. II. The Miracles and Nature—What is the difference between a Miracle and any event in the ordinary course of Nature? III. The Authority of Miracles—Is the Miracle to command absolute obedience? IV. The Evangelical, compared with the other cycles of Miracles. V. The Assaults on the Miracles—*1. *The Jewish.* 2. *The Heathen (Celsus etc.).* 3. *The Pantheistic (Spinoza etc.).* 4. *The Sceptical (Hume).* 5. *The Miracles only relatively miraculous (Schleiermacher).* 6. *The Rationalistic (Paulus).* 7. *The Historico-Critical (Woolston, Strauss). VI. The Apologetic Worth of the Miracles. The author then treats the separate Miracles as he does the Parables.*

### SYNONYMS OF THE NEW TESTAMENT. Eighth Edition, enlarged. 8vo. cloth. 12s.

*This Edition has been carefully revised, and a considerable number of new Synonyms added. Appended is an Index to the Synonyms, and an Index to many other words alluded to or explained throughout the work. "He is," the* Athenæum *says, "a guide in this department of knowledge to whom his readers may intrust themselves with confidence. His sober judgment and sound sense are barriers against the misleading influence of arbitrary hypotheses."*

### ON THE AUTHORIZED VERSION OF THE NEW TESTAMENT. Second Edition. 8vo. 7s.

*After some Introductory Remarks, in which the propriety of a revision is briefly discussed, the whole question of the merits of the present version is gone into in detail, in eleven chapters. Appended is a chronological list of works bearing on the subject, an Index of the principal Texts considered, an Index of Greek Words, and an Index of other Words referred to throughout the book.*

### STUDIES IN THE GOSPELS. Fourth Edition, revised. 8vo. 10s. 6d.

*This book is published under the conviction that the assertion often made is untrue,—viz. that the Gospels are in the main plain and easy,*

**TRENCH (Archbishop)**—*continued.*

and that all the chief difficulties of the New Testament are to be found in the Epistles. These "Studies," sixteen in number, are the fruit of a much larger scheme, and each Study deals with some important episode mentioned in the Gospels, in a critical, philosophical, and practical manner. Many references and quotations are added to the Notes. Among the subjects treated are:—The Temptation; Christ and the Samaritan Woman; The Three Aspirants; The Transfiguration; Zacchæus; The True Vine; The Penitent Malefactor; Christ and the Two Disciples on the way to Emmaus.

**COMMENTARY ON THE EPISTLES to the SEVEN CHURCHES IN ASIA.** Third Edition, revised. 8vo. 8s. 6d.

*The present work consists of an Introduction, being a commentary on Rev. i. 4—20, a detailed examination of each of the Seven Epistles, in all its bearings, and an Excursus on the Historico-Prophetical Interpretation of the Epistles.*

**THE SERMON ON THE MOUNT.** An Exposition drawn from the writings of St. Augustine, with an Essay on his merits as an Interpreter of Holy Scripture. Third Edition, enlarged. 8vo. 10s. 6d.

*The first half of the present work consists of a dissertation in eight chapters on "Augustine as an Interpreter of Scripture," the titles of the several chapters being as follow:—I. Augustine's General Views of Scripture and its Interpretation. II. The External Helps for the Interpretation of Scripture possessed by Augustine. III. Augustine's Principles and Canons of Interpretation. IV. Augustine's Allegorical Interpretation of Scripture. V. Illustrations of Augustine's Skill as an Interpreter of Scripture. VI. Augustine on John the Baptist and on St. Stephen. VII. Augustine on the Epistle to the Romans. VIII. Miscellaneous Examples of Augustine's Interpretation of Scripture. The latter half of the work consists of Augustine's Exposition of the Sermon on the Mount, not however a mere series of quotations from Augustine, but a connected account of his sentiments on the various passages of that Sermon, interspersed with criticisms by Archbishop Trench.*

**SHIPWRECKS OF FAITH.** Three Sermons preached before the University of Cambridge in May, 1867. Fcap. 8vo. 2s. 6d.

*These Sermons are especially addressed to young men. The subjects are "Balaam," "Saul," and "Judas Iscariot." These lives are set forth as beacon-lights, "to warn us off from perilous reefs and quicksands, which have been the destruction of many, and which might only too easily be ours." The* John Bull *says, "they are, like all he writes, affectionate and earnest discourses."*

**TRENCH (Archbishop)**—*continued.*

SERMONS Preached for the most part in Ireland. 8vo. 10s. 6d.

*This volume consists of Thirty-two Sermons, the greater part of which were preached in Ireland; the subjects are as follow:*—*Jacob, a Prince with God and with Men*—*Agrippa*—*The Woman that was a Sinner*—*Secret Faults*—*The Seven Worse Spirits*—*Freedom in the Truth*—*Joseph and his Brethren*—*Bearing one another's Burdens*—*Christ's Challenge to the World*—*The Love of Money*—*The Salt of the Earth*—*The Armour of God*—*Light in the Lord*—*The Jailer of Philippi*—*The Thorn in the Flesh*—*Isaiah's Vision*—*Selfishness*—*Abraham interceding for Sodom*—*Vain Thoughts*—*Pontius Pilate*—*The Brazen Serpent*—*The Death and Burial of Moses*—*A Word from the Cross*—*The Church's Worship in the Beauty of Holiness*—*Every Good Gift from Above*—*On the Hearing of Prayer*—*The Kingdom which cometh not with Observation*—*Pressing towards the Mark*—*Saul*—*The Good Shepherd*—*The Valley of Dry Bones*—*All Saints.*

LECTURES ON MEDIEVAL CHURCH HISTORY. Being the Substance of Lectures delivered in Queen's College, London. Second Edition, revised. 8vo. 12s.

*Contents:*—*The Middle Ages Beginning*—*The Conversion of England*—*Islam*—*The Conversion of Germany*—*The Iconoclasts*—*The Crusades*—*The Papacy at its Height*—*The Sects of the Middle Ages*—*The Mendicant Orders*—*The Waldenses*—*The Revival of Learning*—*Christian Art in the Middle Ages, &c., &c.*

**Tulloch.**—THE CHRIST OF THE GOSPELS AND THE CHRIST OF MODERN CRITICISM. Lectures on M. RENAN's "Vie de Jésus." By JOHN TULLOCH, D.D., Principal of the College of St. Mary, in the University of St. Andrew's. Extra fcap. 8vo. 4s. 6d.

**Vaughan.**—Works by the very Rev. CHARLES JOHN VAUGHAN, D.D., Dean of Llandaff and Master of the Temple:

CHRIST SATISFYING THE INSTINCTS OF HUMANITY. Eight Lectures delivered in the Temple Church. Second Edition. Extra fcap. 8vo. 3s. 6d.

*"We are convinced that there are congregations, in number unmistakably increasing, to whom such Essays as these, full of thought and learning, are infinitely more beneficial, for they are more acceptable, than the recognised type of sermons."*—John Bull.

THE BOOK AND THE LIFE, and other Sermons, preached before the University of Cambridge. Third Edition. Fcap. 8vo. 4s. 6d.

**VAUGHAN (Dr. C. J.)**—*continued.*

**TWELVE DISCOURSES on SUBJECTS CONNECTED WITH THE LITURGY and WORSHIP of the CHURCH OF ENGLAND.** Fcap. 8vo. 6s.

**LESSONS OF LIFE AND GODLINESS.** A Selection of Sermons preached in the Parish Church of Doncaster. Fourth and Cheaper Edition. Fcap. 8vo. 3s. 6d.

*This volume consists of Nineteen Sermons, mostly on subjects connected with the every-day walk and conversation of Christians.* The Spectator *styles them "earnest and human. They are adapted to every class and order in the social system, and will be read with wakeful interest by all who seek to amend whatever may be amiss in their natural disposition or in their acquired habits."*

**WORDS FROM THE GOSPELS.** A Second Selection of Sermons preached in the Parish Church of Doncaster. Third Edition. Fcap. 8vo. 4s. 6d.

*The* Nonconformist *characterises these Sermons as "of practical earnestness, of a thoughtfulness that penetrates the common conditions and experiences of life, and brings the truths and examples of Scripture to bear on them with singular force, and of a style that owes its real elegance to the simplicity and directness which have fine culture for their roots."*

**LIFE'S WORK AND GOD'S DISCIPLINE.** Three Sermons. Third Edition. Fcap. 8vo. 2s. 6d.

**THE WHOLESOME WORDS OF JESUS CHRIST.** Four Sermons preached before the University of Cambridge in November 1866. Second Edition. Fcap. 8vo. 3s. 6d.

*Dr. Vaughan uses the word "Wholesome" here in its literal and original sense, the sense in which St. Paul uses it, as meaning healthy, sound, conducing to right living; and in these Sermons he points out and illustrates several of the "wholesome" characteristics of the Gospel,—the Words of Christ. The* John Bull *says this volume is "replete with all the author's well-known vigour of thought and richness of expression."*

**FOES OF FAITH.** Sermons preached before the University of Cambridge in November 1868. Second Edition. Fcap. 8vo. 3s. 6d.

*The "Foes of Faith" preached against in these Four Sermons are:—I. "Unreality." II. "Indolence." III. "Irreverence." IV. "Inconsistency."*

**LECTURES ON THE EPISTLE to the PHILIPPIANS.** Third and Cheaper Edition. Extra fcap. 8vo. 5s.

*Each Lecture is prefaced by a literal translation from the Greek of the paragraph which forms its subject, contains first a minute explanation*

**VAUGHAN (Dr. C. J.)**—*continued.*
*of the passage on which it is based, and then a practical application of the verse or clause selected as its text.*

### LECTURES ON THE REVELATION OF ST. JOHN.
Fourth Edition. Two Vols. Extra fcap. 8vo. 9s.

*In this Edition of these Lectures, the literal translations of the passages expounded will be found interwoven in the body of the Lectures themselves. "Dr. Vaughan's Sermons," the* Spectator *says, "are the most practical discourses on the Apocalypse with which we are acquainted." Prefixed is a Synopsis of the Book of Revelation, and appended is an Index of passages illustrating the language of the Book.*

### EPIPHANY, LENT, AND EASTER.
A Selection of Expository Sermons. Third Edition. Crown 8vo. 10s. 6d.

### THE EPISTLES OF ST. PAUL.
For English Readers. PART I., containing the FIRST EPISTLE TO THE THESSALONIANS. Second Edition. 8vo. 1s. 6d.

*It is the object of this work to enable English readers, unacquainted with Greek, to enter with intelligence into the meaning, connection, and phraseology of the writings of the great Apostle.*

### ST. PAUL'S EPISTLE TO THE ROMANS.
The Greek Text, with English Notes. Fourth Edition. Crown 8vo. 7s. 6d.

*The* Guardian *says of the work,—"For educated young men his commentary seems to fill a gap hitherto unfilled.... As a whole, Dr. Vaughan appears to us to have given to the world a valuable book of original and careful and earnest thought bestowed on the accomplishment of a work which will be of much service and which is much needed."*

### THE CHURCH OF THE FIRST DAYS.
Series I. The Church of Jerusalem. Third Edition.
" II. The Church of the Gentiles. Third Edition.
" III. The Church of the World. Third Edition.
Fcap. 8vo. 4s. 6d. each.

*The* British Quarterly *says, "These Sermons are worthy of all praise, and are models of pulpit teaching."*

### COUNSELS for YOUNG STUDENTS.
Three Sermons preached before the University of Cambridge at the Opening of the Academical Year 1870-71. Fcap. 8vo. 2s. 6d.

*The titles of the Three Sermons contained in this volume are:—I. "The Great Decision." II. "The House and the Builder." III. "The Prayer and the Counter-Prayer." They all bear pointedly, earnestly, and sympathisingly upon the conduct and pursuits of young students and young men generally.*

**VAUGHAN (Dr. C. J.)**—*continued.*

NOTES FOR LECTURES ON CONFIRMATION, with suitable Prayers. Tenth Edition. Fcap. 8vo. 1s. 6d.

THE TWO GREAT TEMPTATIONS. The Temptation of Man, and the Temptation of Christ. Lectures delivered in the Temple Church, Lent 1872. Second Edition. Extra fcap. 8vo. 3s. 6d.

WORDS FROM THE CROSS: Lent Lectures, 1875; and Thoughts for these Times: University Sermons, 1874. Extra fcap. 8vo. 4s. 6d.

ADDRESSES TO YOUNG CLERGYMEN, delivered at Salisbury in September and October, 1875. Extra fcap. 8vo. 4s. 6d.

HEROES OF FAITH: Lectures on Hebrews xi. Extra fcap. 8vo. 6s.

THE YOUNG LIFE EQUIPPING ITSELF FOR GOD'S SERVICE: Sermons before the University of Cambridge. Sixth Edition. Extra fcap. 8vo. 3s. 6d.

THE SOLIDITY OF TRUE RELIGION; and other Sermons. Second Edition. Extra fcap. 8vo. 3s. 6d.

SERMONS IN HARROW SCHOOL CHAPEL (1847). 8vo. 10s. 6d.

NINE SERMONS IN HARROW SCHOOL CHAPEL (1849). Fcap. 8vo. 5s.

"MY SON, GIVE ME THINE HEART," SERMONS Preached before the Universities of Oxford and Cambridge, 1876—78. Fcap. 8vo. 5s.

**Vaughan (E. T.)**—SOME REASONS OF OUR CHRISTIAN HOPE. Hulsean Lectures for 1875. By E. T. VAUGHAN, M.A., Rector of Harpenden. Crown 8vo. 6s. 6d.

"*His words are those of a well-tried scholar and a sound theologian, and they will be read widely and valued deeply by an audience far beyond the range of that which listened to their masterly pleading at Cambridge.*" —Standard.

**Vaughan (D. J.)**—Works by CANON VAUGHAN, of Leicester:

SERMONS PREACHED IN ST. JOHN'S CHURCH, LEICESTER, during the Years 1855 and 1856. Cr. 8vo. 5s. 6d.

## THEOLOGICAL BOOKS.

**VAUGHAN (D. J.)**—*continued.*

CHRISTIAN EVIDENCES AND THE BIBLE. New Edition, revised and enlarged. Fcap. 8vo. cloth. 5s. 6d.

THE PRESENT TRIAL OF FAITH. Sermons preached in St. Martin's Church, Leicester. Crown 8vo. 9s.

**Venn.**—ON SOME OF THE CHARACTERISTICS OF BELIEF, Scientific and Religious. Being the Hulsean Lectures for 1869. By the Rev. J. VENN, M.A. 8vo. 6s. 6d.

*These discourses are intended to illustrate, explain, and work out into some of their consequences, certain characteristics by which the attainment of religious belief is prominently distinguished from the attainment of belief upon most other subjects.*

**Warington.**—THE WEEK OF CREATION; or, The Cosmogony of Genesis considered in its Relation to Modern Science. By GEORGE WARINGTON, Author of "The Historic Character of the Pentateuch vindicated." Crown 8vo. 4s. 6d.

*"A very able vindication of the Mosaic Cosmogony by a writer who unites the advantages of a critical knowledge of the Hebrew text and of distinguished scientific attainments."*—Spectator.

**Westcott.**—Works by BROOKE FOSS WESTCOTT, D.D., Regius Professor of Divinity in the University of Cambridge; Canon of Peterborough:

*The* London Quarterly, *speaking of Mr. Westcott, says, "To a learning and accuracy which command respect and confidence, he unites what are not always to be found in union with these qualities, the no less valuable faculties of lucid arrangement and graceful and facile expression."*

AN INTRODUCTION TO THE STUDY OF THE GOSPELS. Fifth Edition. Crown 8vo. 10s. 6d.

*The author's chief object in this work has been to shew that there is a true mean between the idea of a formal harmonization of the Gospels and the abandonment of their absolute truth. After an Introduction on the General Effects of the course of Modern Philosophy on the popular views of Christianity, he proceeds to determine in what way the principles therein indicated may be applied to the study of the Gospels.*

A GENERAL SURVEY OF THE HISTORY OF THE CANON OF THE NEW TESTAMENT during the First Four Centuries. Fourth Edition, revised, with a Preface on "Supernatural Religion." Crown 8vo. 10s. 6d.

*The object of this treatise is to deal with the New Testament as a whole, and that on purely historical grounds. The separate books of which it is*

**WESTCOTT (Dr.)**—*continued.*

composed are considered not individually, but as claiming to be parts of the apostolic heritage of Christians. The Author has thus endeavoured to connect the history of the New Testament Canon with the growth and consolidation of the Catholic Church, and to point out the relation existing between the amount of evidence for the authenticity of its component parts and the whole mass of Christian literature. *"The treatise,"* says the British Quarterly, *"is a scholarly performance, learned, dispassionate, discriminating, worthy of his subject and of the present state of Christian literature in relation to it."*

**THE BIBLE IN THE CHURCH.** A Popular Account of the Collection and Reception of the Holy Scriptures in the Christian Churches. Sixth Edition. 18mo. 4s. 6d.

**A GENERAL VIEW OF THE HISTORY OF THE ENGLISH BIBLE.** Second Edition. Crown 8vo. 10s. 6d.

*The Pall Mall Gazette calls the work "A brief, scholarly, and, to a great extent, an original contribution to theological literature."*

**THE CHRISTIAN LIFE, MANIFOLD AND ONE.** Six Sermons preached in Peterborough Cathedral. Crown 8vo. 2s. 6d.

*The Six Sermons contained in this volume are the first preached by the author as a Canon of Peterborough Cathedral. The subjects are:—I. "Life consecrated by the Ascension." II. "Many Gifts, One Spirit." III. "The Gospel of the Resurrection." IV. "Sufficiency of God." V. "Action the Test of Faith." VI. "Progress from the Confession of God."*

**THE GOSPEL OF THE RESURRECTION.** Thoughts on its Relation to Reason and History. Third Edition, enlarged. Crown 8vo. 6s.

*The present Essay is an endeavour to consider some of the elementary truths of Christianity, as a miraculous Revelation, from the side of History and Reason. The author endeavours to shew that a devout belief in the Life of Christ is quite compatible with a broad view of the course of human progress and a frank trust in the laws of our own minds. In the third edition the author has carefully reconsidered the whole argument, and by the help of several kind critics has been enabled to correct some faults and to remove some ambiguities, which had been overlooked before.*

**ON THE RELIGIOUS OFFICE OF THE UNIVERSITIES.** Crown 8vo. 4s. 6d.

*"There is certainly no man of our time—no man at least who has obtained the command of the public ear—whose utterances can compare with those of Professor Westcott for largeness of views and comprehensiveness of*

*grasp......There is wisdom, and truth, and thought enough, and a harmony and mutual connection running through them all, which makes the collection of more real value than many an ambitious treatise."—*Literary Churchman.

**Wilkins.**—THE LIGHT OF THE WORLD. An Essay, by A. S. WILKINS, M.A., Professor of Latin in Owens College, Manchester. Second Edition. Crown 8vo. 3s. 6d.

"*It would be difficult to praise too highly the spirit, the burden, the conclusions, or the scholarly finish of this beautiful Essay.*"—British Quarterly Review.

**Wilson.**—THE BIBLE STUDENT'S GUIDE TO THE MORE CORRECT UNDERSTANDING of the ENGLISH TRANSLATION OF THE OLD TESTAMENT, by Reference to the Original Hebrew. By WILLIAM WILSON, D.D., Canon of Winchester. Second Edition, carefully revised. 4to. 25s.

"*The author believes that the present work is the nearest approach to a complete Concordance of every word in the original that has yet been made: and as a Concordance, it may be found of great use to the Bible student, while at the same time it serves the important object of furnishing the means of comparing synonymous words, and of eliciting their precise and distinctive meaning. The knowledge of the Hebrew language is not absolutely necessary to the profitable use of the work. The plan of the work is simple: every word occurring in the English Version is arranged alphabetically, and under it is given the Hebrew word or words, with a full explanation of their meaning, of which it is meant to be a translation, and a complete list of the passages where it occurs. Following the general work is a complete Hebrew and English Index, which is, in effect, a Hebrew-English Dictionary.*

**Worship (The) of God and Fellowship among Men.** Sermons on Public Worship. By Professor MAURICE, and others. Fcap. 8vo. 3s. 6d.

**Yonge (Charlotte M.)**—Works by CHARLOTTE M. YONGE, Author of "The Heir of Redclyffe:"

SCRIPTURE READINGS FOR SCHOOLS AND FAMILIES. 5 vols. Globe 8vo. 1s. 6d. With Comments, 3s. 6d. each.

FIRST SERIES. Genesis to Deuteronomy.
SECOND SERIES. From Joshua to Solomon.
THIRD SERIES. The Kings and Prophets.
FOURTH SERIES. The Gospel Times.
FIFTH SERIES. Apostolic Times.

**YONGE (Charlotte M.)**—*continued.*

*Actual need has led the author to endeavour to prepare a reading book convenient for study with children, containing the very words of the Bible, with only a few expedient omissions, and arranged in Lessons of such length as by experience she has found to suit with children's ordinary power of accurate attentive interest. The verse form has been retained because of its convenience for children reading in class, and as more resembling their Bibles; but the poetical portions have been given in their lines. Professor Huxley at a meeting of the London School-board, particularly mentioned the Selection made by Miss Yonge, as an example of how selections might be made for School reading. " Her Comments are models of their kind."*—Literary Churchman.

**THE PUPILS OF ST. JOHN THE DIVINE.** New Edition. Crown 8vo. 6s.

"*Young and old will be equally refreshed and taught by these pages, in which nothing is dull, and nothing is far-fetched.*"—Churchman.

**PIONEERS AND FOUNDERS;** or, Recent Workers in the Mission Field. With Frontispiece and Vignette Portrait of Bishop HEBER. Crown 8vo. 6s.

*The missionaries whose biographies are here given, are—John Eliot, the Apostle of the Red Indians; David Brainerd, the Enthusiast; Christian F. Schwartz, the Councillor of Tanjore; Henry Martyn, the Scholar-Missionary; William Carey and Joshua Marshman, the Serampore Missionaries; the Judson Family; the Bishops of Calcutta—Thomas Middleton, Reginald Heber, Daniel Wilson; Samuel Marsden, the Australian Chaplain and Friend of the Maori; John Williams, the Martyr of Erromango; Allen Gardener, the Sailor Martyr; Charles Frederick Mackenzie, the Martyr of Zambesi.*

# THE "BOOK OF PRAISE" HYMNAL,
### COMPILED AND ARRANGED BY
## LORD SELBORNE.

*In the following four forms:—*

A. Beautifully printed in Royal 32mo., limp cloth, price 6d.
B.    ,,         ,,    Small 18mo., larger type, cloth limp, 1s.
C. Same edition on fine paper, cloth, 1s. 6d.
Also an edition with Music, selected, harmonized, and composed by JOHN HULLAH, in square 18mo., cloth, 3s. 6d.

*The large acceptance which has been given to "The Book of Praise" by all classes of Christian people encourages the Publishers in entertaining the hope that this Hymnal, which is mainly selected from it, may be extensively used in Congregations, and in some degree at least meet the desires of those who seek uniformity in common worship as a means towards that unity which pious souls yearn after, and which our Lord prayed for in behalf of his Church. "The office of a hymn is not to teach controversial Theology, but to give the voice of song to practical religion. No doubt, to do this, it must embody sound doctrine; but it ought to do so, not after the manner of the schools, but with the breadth, freedom, and simplicity of the Fountain-head." On this principle has Sir R. Palmer proceeded in the preparation of this book.*

The arrangement adopted is the following:—

PART I. *consists of Hymns arranged according to the subjects of the Creed*—"*God the Creator*," "*Christ Incarnate*," "*Christ Crucified*," "*Christ Risen*," "*Christ Ascended*," "*Christ's Kingdom and Judgment*," *etc.*

PART II. *comprises Hymns arranged according to the subjects of the Lord's Prayer.*

PART III. *Hymns for natural and sacred seasons.*

*There are* 320 *Hymns in all.*

---

CAMBRIDGE:—PRINTED BY J. PALMER.

www.ingramcontent.com/pod-product-compliance
Lightning Source LLC
Chambersburg PA
CBHW022111160426
43197CB00009B/985